THE GLOBAL PARTNE
FOR ENVIRONMENT AND DE

The Global Partnership
for Environment and Development

A Guide to Agenda 21
Post Rio Edition

United Nations · New York 1993

THE *progress made so far in reaching agreement on Agenda 21 is a remarkable achievement. It demonstrates universal goodwill as well as the importance attached to this ambitious instrument. Agenda 21 will remain a key point of reference for the rest of the decade for Governments and international organizations, as well as the non-governmental community and the public at large . . . I see this as the centrepiece of international cooperation and of coordination of activities within the United Nations system for many years to come.*

Boutros Boutros-Ghali
Secretary-General • United Nations
June 1992

FOREWORD

HUMANITY is confronted with deepening disparities within and between nations. There is pervasive hunger, poverty, illiteracy and ill health. The ecological consequences of ozone depletion, climate change, soil degradation, deforestation, loss of biodiversity, and the increasing pollution of air, water and land threaten our common and sustainable future. The urgency of these development and environment concerns prompted the nations of the world, in resolution 44/228 of the United Nations General Assembly, to convene a United Nations Conference on Environment and Development in Rio de Janeiro, Brazil, in June of 1992.

A principal outcome of the Rio Conference is Agenda 21, an action plan for the 1990s and the 21st century, elaborating strategies and integrated programme measures to halt and reverse the effects of the environmental degradation and to promote environmentally sound and sustainable development in all countries. This Agenda comprises some 40 chapters and totals over 800 pages. It is the product of intense negotiations among Governments on the basis of proposals prepared by the secretariat of the United Nations Conference on Environment and Development, drawing on extensive inputs from relevant United Nations agencies and organizations, expert consultations, intergovernmental and non-governmental organizations, regional conferences and national reports, and the direction provided through four sessions of the Preparatory Committee of the Conference.

We have prepared this summary guide to Agenda 21 within a framework of principal social themes, such as the revitalization of growth with sustainability, sustainable living for all and the development of human settlements for a world that is prospering, just and habitable. This involves the sustainable and efficient use of all resources and the proper management of pollution and waste through a wide and responsible participation of people at the local, national and global levels. The successful implementation of Agenda 21 necessitates a global partnership for sustainable development within which all nations make political, social and economic commitments, individually and collectively, to ensure the allocation of essential means for a viable and sustainable human future.

Agenda 21 is based on the premise that sustainable development is not just an option but an imperative, in both environmental and economic terms, and that while the transition to sustainable development will be difficult, it is entirely feasible. It requires a major shift in priorities for governments and people, involving the full integration of the environmental dimension into economic policies and decision-making in every sphere of activity and a major redeployment of human and financial resources at national and international levels. This global partnership is essential to set the world community onto a new course for a more sustainable, secure and equitable future as we prepare ourselves for the 21st century. The need to commit ourselves to a common future is, in a very real sense, "in our hands".

Maurice F. Strong
Secretary-General
United Nations Conference on Environment
and Development • April 1992

NOTE TO FOREWORD

THE United Nations Conference on Environment and Development in Rio de Janeiro last June was a unique and historic event. It brought 118 Heads of State and Government together, making it the largest and most complex summit meeting ever held, as well as the first truly Earth Summit.

In concrete terms, the Rio Conference mobilized Governments to move the environment issue firmly to the centre of development planning, and of economic and sectoral policy and decision-making. It witnessed the endorsement of an important political framework for the Agenda 21 action programmes, the Rio Declaration on Environment and Development, which places people at the core of our concerns for a sustainable future; the signing of two legally-binding treaties—the Convention on Biological Diversity and the United Nations Framework Convention on Climate Change—by 153 Member States of the United Nations and the European Economic Community; the ratification of a Statement of Principles for the Conservation of Forests; the agreement to set up a high-level Commission on Sustainable Development to translate the achievements of Rio into immediate practical action; and the commitment of nations to the transfer of technology and the provision of new and additional financial resources.

A key product of the Earth Summit is the Agenda 21. This is an agreed programme of cooperative international work for the sustained and responsible development of our planet as we prepare ourselves for the challenges of the 21st century. Agenda 21 reflects a global consensus and political commitment at the highest level on environment and development cooperation and, with its emphasis on environment *and* development, highlights the integrative nature of the Rio process.

This concise guide to Agenda 21 incorporates the amendments made in Rio de Janeiro. The original version of this guide was prepared by Dr. Mahendra Shah. Revisions in the present version were prepared by Sajid Alikhan. I am grateful to both of them for their efforts to make the Agenda 21 accessible to a wider audience.

Nitin Desai
Deputy Secretary-General
United Nations Conference on Environment
and Development • September 1992

CONTENTS

Foreword vii
Note to Foreword ix

I
THE RIO DECLARATION
ON ENVIRONMENT AND DEVELOPMENT   1

II
AGENDA 21: AN OVERVIEW   11

III
AGENDA 21: THE PRIORITY ACTIONS   39

1 *Revitalizing growth with sustainability*   43
1.1 International cooperation to accelerate sustainable development in developing countries and related domestic policies   48
1.2 Integrating environment and development in decision-making   51

2 *Sustainable living*   56
2.1 Combating poverty   57
2.2 Changing consumption patterns   63
2.3 Demographic dynamics and sustainability   67
2.4 Protecting and promoting human health conditions   71

3 *Human settlements*   76
3.1 Promoting sustainable human settlement development   81
3.2 Urban water supplies   85

3.3	Environmentally sound management of solid wastes and sewage-related issues	88
3.4	Urban pollution and health	91
4	*Efficient resource use*	95
4.1	Integrated approach to the planning and management of land resources	101
4.2	Protection of the quality and supply of freshwater resources: Application of integrated approaches to the development, management and use of water resources	104
4.3	Promoting sustainable agriculture and rural development	108
4.4	Combating deforestation	113
4.5	Managing fragile ecosystems	117
4.5.1	Combating desertification and drought	118
4.5.2	Sustainable mountain development	120
4.5.3	Protection of coastal areas	123
4.5.4	Sustainable development of islands	125
4.6	Conservation of biological diversity	127
4.7	Environmentally sound management of biotechnology	129
5	*Global and regional resources*	134
5.1	Protection of the atmosphere	139
5.2	Protection of the oceans and all kinds of seas, including enclosed and semi-enclosed seas	143
5.3	Protection, rational use and development of living marine resources	148
6	*Managing chemicals and wastes*	153
6.1	Environmentally sound management of toxic chemicals, including prevention of illegal international traffic in toxic and dangerous products	158

6.2 Environmentally sound management of hazardous wastes, including prevention of illegal international traffic in hazardous wastes 162
6.3 Safe and environmentally sound management of radioactive wastes 165

7 *People's participation and responsibility* 167
7.1 Promoting education, public awareness and training 172
7.2 Strengthening the role of major groups 176
7.2.1 Global action for women towards sustainable and equitable development 176
7.2.2 Children and youth in sustainable development . . 179
7.2.3 Recognizing and strengthening the role of indigenous people and their communities 181
7.2.4 Strengthening the role of non-governmental organizations: partners for sustainable development 183
7.2.5 Strengthening the role of farmers 184
7.2.6 Local authorities' initiatives in support of Agenda 21 186
7.2.7 Strengthening the role of workers and their trade unions 188
7.2.8 Strengthening the role of business and industry . . . 189
7.2.9 Scientific and technological community 191

IV

AGENDA 21: THE ESSENTIAL MEANS   195

8 *Information for decision-making* 201

9 *National mechanisms and international cooperation for capacity-building* 205

10 *Science for sustainable development* 209

11 *Transfer of environmentally sound technology, cooperation and capacity-building* 213

12 *International legal instruments and mechanisms* . . 216

13 *International institutional arrangements* 219

14 *Financial resources and mechanisms* 223

V

NON-LEGALLY BINDING AUTHORITATIVE
STATEMENT OF PRINCIPLES FOR A
GLOBAL CONSENSUS ON THE MANAGEMENT,
CONSERVATION AND SUSTAINABLE DEVELOPMENT
OF ALL TYPES OF FORESTS   227

I

The Rio Declaration on Environment and Development

THE RIO DECLARATION ON ENVIRONMENT AND DEVELOPMENT

PREAMBLE

THE United Nations Conference on Environment and Development,

Having met at Rio de Janeiro from 3 to 14 June 1992,
Reaffirming the Declaration of the United Nations Conference on the Human Environment, adopted at Stockholm on 16 June 1972, and seeking to build upon it,
With the goal of establishing a new and equitable global partnership through the creation of new levels of cooperation among States, key sectors of societies and people,
Working towards international agreements which respect the interests of all and protect the integrity of the global environmental and developmental system,
Recognizing the integral and interdependent nature of the Earth, our home,
Proclaims that:

Principle 1

Human beings are at the centre of concerns for sustainable development. They are entitled to a healthy and productive life in harmony with nature.

Principle 2

States have, in accordance with the Charter of the United Nations and the principles of international law, the sovereign right to exploit their own resources pursuant to their own environmental and developmental policies, and the responsibility to ensure that activities within their jurisdiction or control do not cause damage to the environment of other States or of areas beyond the limits of national jurisdiction.

Principle 3

The right to development must be fulfilled so as to equitably meet developmental and environmental needs of present and future generations.

Principle 4

In order to achieve sustainable development, environmental protection shall constitute an integral part of the development process and cannot be considered in isolation from it.

Principle 5

All States and all people shall cooperate in the essential task of eradicating poverty as an indispensable requirement for sustainable development, in order to decrease the disparities in standards of living and better meet the needs of the majority of the people of the world.

Principle 6

The special situation and needs of developing countries, particularly the least developed and those most environmentally vulnerable, shall be given special priority. International actions in the field of environment and development should also address the interests and needs of all countries.

Principle 7

States shall cooperate in a spirit of global partnership to conserve, protect and restore the health and integrity of the Earth's ecosystem. In view of the different contributions to global environmental degradation, States have common but differentiated responsibilities. The developed countries acknowledge the responsibility that they bear in the international pursuit of sustainable development in view of the pressures their societies place on the global environment and of the technologies and financial resources they command.

Principle 8

To achieve sustainable development and a higher quality of life for all people, States should reduce and eliminate unsustainable patterns of production and consumption and promote appropriate demographic policies.

Principle 9

States should cooperate to strengthen endogenous capacity-building for sustainable development by improving scientific understanding through exchanges of scientific and technological knowledge, and by enhancing the development, adaptation, diffusion and transfer of technologies, including new and innovative technologies.

Principle 10

Environmental issues are best handled with the participation of all concerned citizens, at the relevant level. At the national level, each individual shall have appropriate access to information concerning the environment that is held by public authorities, including information on hazardous materials and activities in their communities, and the opportunity to participate in decision-making processes. States shall facilitate and encourage public awareness and participation by making information widely available. Effective access to judicial and administrative proceedings, including redress and remedy, shall be provided.

Principle 11
States shall enact effective environmental legislation. Environmental standards, management objectives and priorities should reflect the environmental and developmental context to which they apply. Standards applied by some countries may be inappropriate and of unwarranted economic and social cost to other countries, in particular developing countries.

Principle 12
States should cooperate to promote a supportive and open international economic system that would lead to economic growth and sustainable development in all countries, to better address the problems of environmental degradation. Trade policy measures for environmental purposes should not constitute a means of arbitrary or unjustifiable discrimination or a disguised restriction on international trade. Unilateral actions to deal with environmental challenges outside the jurisdiction of the importing country should be avoided. Environmental measures addressing transboundary or global environmental problems should, as far as possible, be based on an international consensus.

Principle 13
States shall develop national law regarding liability and compensation for the victims of pollution and other environmental damage. States shall also cooperate in an expeditious and more determined manner to develop further international law regarding liability and compensation for adverse effects of environmental damage caused by activities within their jurisdiction or control to areas beyond their jurisdiction.

Principle 14
States should effectively cooperate to discourage or prevent the relocation and transfer to other States of any activities and substances that cause severe environmental degradation or are found to be harmful to human health.

Principle 15
In order to protect the environment, the precautionary approach shall be widely applied by States according to their capabilities. Where there are threats of serious or irreversible damage, lack of full scientific certainty shall not be used as a reason for postponing cost-effective measures to prevent environmental degradation.

Principle 16
National authorities should endeavour to promote the internalization of environmental costs and the use of economic instruments, taking into account the approach that the polluter should, in principle, bear the cost of pollution, with due regard to the public interest and without distorting international trade and investment.

Principle 17
Environmental impact assessment, as a national instrument, shall be undertaken for proposed activities that are likely to have a significant adverse impact on the environment and are subject to a decision of a competent national authority.

Principle 18
States shall immediately notify other States of any natural disasters or other emergencies that are likely to produce sudden harmful effects on the environment of those States. Every effort shall be made by the international community to help States so afflicted.

Principle 19
States shall provide prior and timely notification and relevant information to potentially affected States on activities that may have a significant adverse transboundary environmental effect and shall consult with those States at an early stage and in good faith.

Principle 20
Women have a vital role in environmental management and development. Their full participation is therefore essential to achieve sustainable development.

Principle 21
The creativity, ideals and courage of the youth of the world should be mobilized to forge a global partnership in order to achieve sustainable development and ensure a better future for all.

Principle 22
Indigenous people and their communities, and other local communities, have a vital role in environmental management and development because of their knowledge and traditional practices. States should recognize and duly support their identity, culture and interests and enable their effective participation in the achievement of sustainable development.

Principle 23
The environment and natural resources of people under oppression, domination and occupation shall be protected.

Principle 24
Warfare is inherently destructive of sustainable development. States shall therefore respect international law providing protection for the environment in times of armed

conflict and cooperate in its further development, as necessary.

Principle 25
Peace, development and environmental protection are interdependent and indivisible.

Principle 26
States shall resolve all their environmental disputes peacefully and by appropriate means in accordance with the Charter of the United Nations.

Principle 27
States and people shall cooperate in good faith and in a spirit of partnership in the fulfilment of the principles embodied in this Declaration and in the further development of international law in the field of sustainable development.

II

*Agenda 21:
An Overview*

II

AGENDA 21:
AN OVERVIEW

ON the 22nd of December 1989, at its 85th plenary meeting, the United Nations General Assembly resolved to convene a United Nations Conference on Environment and Development in Rio de Janeiro, Brazil, and urged that representation at the Conference be at the level of head of State or Government.

Achieving sustainable development and environmental protection are both priority issues that affect economic growth and the well-being of peoples throughout the world. For the past two decades—ever since the United Nations Conference on the Human Environment in Stockholm in 1972—concern has mounted over the continuing deterioration of the environment and the lack of adequate development in developing countries.

Upsetting the Earth's fine ecological balance augurs badly for our small planet, threatening its life-sustaining qualities and eventually leading to ecological and economic catastrophe. Environmental destruction has resulted principally from the unsustainable patterns of production and consumption in industrialized countries, where the major proportion of the world's current emission of pollutants and toxic and hazardous wastes is produced. The industrialized countries possess the capacity, and the main responsibility, to combat the global effects of this pollution.

The development gap between industrialized and developing nations has widened over the last few decades. The number of people living in poverty has not diminished. More than 1 billion people in the developing world today live without adequate food, health care, education and housing. In calling for a Conference on Environment and Development, Member States of the United Nations stressed that poverty and environmental degradation were interrelated and that environmental protection in developing countries had to be seen as an integral part of their economic growth.

This is not a new concept. It was memorably articulated in the 1987 report of the World Commission on Environment and Development, which recognized that international environmental protection measures have to take current global imbalances in production and consumption fully into account and that addressing environmental problems in industrialized and developing countries required an integration of environmentally sound and sustainable development.

The mandate of the United Nations Conference on Environment and Development emanates from resolution 44/228 of the United Nations General Assembly. In this resolution, Member States agreed that the global character of the environmental problems they faced—climate change, stratospheric ozone depletion, transboundary air and water pollution, contamination of oceans and seas—called for a vigorous response at all levels, on a national and global scale. They stressed the need for effective international cooperation in researching, developing and applying environmentally sound technologies. They also recognized that this global effort would require a supportive international economic climate conducive to sustained economic growth and development in all countries. This would involve channelling new and additional financial resources and providing favourable access to science and technology to all developing countries to ensure their full participation in furthering global environmental protection efforts. Special attention was to be given to developing countries with serious debt-servicing problems.

It was also agreed that countries whose actions harmed the global environment bore primary responsibility for redressing the damage. States retained their sovereign right to develop their own resources pursuant to their own policies; nevertheless, their activities must not environmentally damage other States or areas beyond their jurisdiction. States would also be held responsible for environmental damage to others from sources within their jurisdiction or control.

The General Assembly decided that the Conference should elaborate strategies and measures to halt and reverse the effects of environmental degradation and promote sustainable and environmentally sound development in all countries.

These strategies and measures are embodied in Agenda 21, the centrepiece of the agreement that emerged from the United Nations Conference on Environment and Development in Rio de Janeiro, Brazil, in June of 1992. In adopting Agenda 21, the Rio Conference formally recognized that the integration of environment and development is a comprehensive, dynamic and wide-ranging action process to be undertaken by the world community and involving a wide cast of actors at the international, regional and national level.

Agenda 21, as the basis for action by the international community to integrate environment and development, is a blueprint for a global partnership for the period beyond 1992 and into the 21st century. It is a bold mandate for change, a call for a fundamental reform in our economic behaviour, based on a new understanding and awareness of the impact of human activity on the environment. Agenda 21 underscores the need for a new universal partnership for sustainable development and environmental protection in an increasingly interdependent world. This cooperation should go beyond the traditional notion of "foreign aid", which is no longer an adequate basis for relationships between rich and poor nations.

A new multilateralism is called for, founded on common interests, mutual needs and common but differentiated responsibilities, one where developing countries would have the incentive as well as the means to cooperate fully in protecting the global environment and at the same time meeting their aspirations for economic growth. For this global partnership to be effective, it must be accompanied by new levels of cooperation between all key sectors of society and Government.

The last decade of the 20th century offers a unique opportunity for the world community to make the transition to a sustainable living for all. The end of the Cold War, the world-wide thrust for democracy and other recent political events have created an enabling environment that can generate the means and political will to effect fundamental changes for the transition to a sustainable society. If these changes do not occur now, the cumulative damage from unsustainable actions will make it ever harder for future generations to come to terms with a degraded living environment. It is essential that this transition to sustainable development be initiated immediately and be managed cooperatively by all the main actors shaping the future of our world.

Agenda 21 speaks to Governments, to the United Nations agencies, organizations and programmes, to other intergovernmental and non-governmental organizations, to constituency groups and to the public at large, all of which must be involved, in various ways, in its implementation. These programmes are grouped around a series of themes, each of which represents an important dimension of an overall strategy for global transition.

* * *

The first theme is the *revitalization of growth with sustainability*. The causes of most environmental problems in the world have their origins in the development process, or in its failures and inadequacies, and it is only through better management of this process that these problems can be addressed. Equally, environmental considerations impose new constraints upon traditional modes and patterns of development.

Many people throughout the world have been affected in recent years by declining or stagnating incomes, deteriorating infrastructure and public services, increasing pollution and health hazards and a gradual loss of economic resilience in the face of internal or external shocks. The deterioration in the developing world is of particular concern in view of the persisting and debilitating poverty which severely affects more than 1 billion people. All underlying causes of development failures need to be corrected if the transition to sustainability is to be effectively implemented.

The integration of development and environment at all levels of political and economic decision-making is essential to ensure sustainability. The system of incentives and penalties which motivates economic behaviour must be reoriented to become a strong force for sustainability, and changes in national accounting must reflect the real values of the environment and natural resources. The transition to sustainability requires a much more effective use of resources, as well as greater accountability for the environmental and economic impacts of such use. This requires a balance between regulatory measures and economic incentives. It is fully consistent with market economy principles for the value of economic transactions and products to reflect their full costs, including environmental costs. The operation of market forces can, and must, act as a powerful stimulant for change. This system of incentives and penalties must be re-examined and reoriented to help realize the transition to sustainability in both societal and individual behaviour.

National policies and development projects will have to take full account of their effects on the environment and include the cost of natural resource depletion in the value of environmental quality in national accounting systems. Internalizing environmental costs has special implications for international trade. When the industrialized world imports products from developing countries at costs which do not reflect the destruction of their natural capital, this essentially exacts an environmental subsidy which impoverishes the developing countries' resource base and contributes to global environmental deterioration. At the same time, unilaterally imposed restrictions on imports to meet developed countries' requirements result in immediate and often critical damage to vulnerable developing economies. These problems can be resolved only through international agreements which respect the interests of all parties and protect the integrity of the global environmental and developmental system.

Over the last decade, developing countries which depend on primary commodity exports have encountered a substantial fall in the prices of many non-fuel commodities in real terms. This has severely affected the foreign exchange earnings of these countries. In addition, the availability of these underpriced commodities in industrialized countries may have contributed to their wasteful consumption patterns. Trade policy instruments have a potentially major role to play in ensuring that the price of all traded products reflects the full value of natural resources, including their contribution towards maintaining environmental quality. Improvements in the international trade system are, therefore, critical to reaching sustainable development. The industrialized and developing countries have a common interest in ensuring that trade and environmental policies are mutually supportive.

Developing countries cannot be expected to make the transition to sustainability without the support of the international community. This is particularly necessary to reverse the outflow of resources that has stifled their economic growth and to ensure that they have long-term access to the resource flows that are needed to revitalize their economic life and make the transition to environmentally sustainable development. Of critical importance in this respect is the need to deal more fundamentally with the issue of debt. "Debt-for-nature" swaps may be useful in addressing particular needs, but are marginal in their overall effect. The principle, however, of basic reduction in debt-servicing charges is essential to the revitalization of development.

Development has more than utilitarian purposes. It is rooted in the deepest moral, ethical and spiritual motivations of people and must respond to their fundamental values.

These issues form the vital elements in achieving a *Prospering World*, through the Agenda 21 programmes for accelerated sustainable growth.

* * *

The human condition and aspirations for a better future continue to be thwarted in large parts of the world by a crippling combination of poverty, malnutrition, demographic pressure, unemployment, lack of health care, wasteful uses of energy, pollution, and destruction of natural resources and life-support systems—the air, water, land and forest.

A dual approach, combining poverty alleviation with changes in the lifestyles of the rich to those that are less polluting and wasteful, is essential for sustainable development. Addressing these twin problems of non-sustainable consumption and debilitating poverty would involve significant changes in lifestyles: more people in the industrialized world would opt for lives of sophisticated modesty, while the inhabitants of developing nations would receive greater support in their attempts to achieve livelihoods that do not undermine or destroy the environment and resource base upon which they rely. This would necessitate basic changes in consumer preference and practice, the portents of which are increasingly visible in the trend towards greener consumerism. It will also involve renewed efforts by developing countries to bring the benefits of development to their entire populations and more catalytic support by the international community.

The overall level, pattern and distribution of consumption and production must be compatible with the capacities of the life-support systems of the globe. Excessive global consumption, along with rapidly burgeoning populations, is threatening the basic integrity of fragile ecoystems at local, national and global levels, as well as the survival and well-being of all, rich and poor.

Development and the environment are fundamentally affected by population variables, critical factors that influence consumption patterns, production, lifestyles and long-term sustainability. Greater attention has to be given to these issues in general policy formulation and the design of sustainable options. All countries need to improve their capacities to assess the environmental and developmental implications of their population growth rates and distribution patterns and to formulate and implement appropriate policies and action programmes.

The depletion of resources, the pollution of air, land and water and changes in hydrological regimes and vegetation cover have had deleterious effects on the health and lives of millions of people. Health and disease patterns in developing countries are often determined by poverty. Health and sustainable development are not only interdependent but reciprocal: the achievement of health for all, in accordance with the principle of primary health care, requires sustainable social and economic development, the sustainable use of natural resources for reliable food supplies and energy, healthy cities and the prevention of environmental health risks from the development process itself.

The fundamental imperative is to achieve *sustainable living* for people all over the world, and for future generations. This second theme of a _Just World_ entails coordinated actions to substantially reduce—and ultimately eradicate—poverty worldwide, to ensure healthy and equitable livelihoods for all and to achieve global consumption pattern levels which help mitigate environmental damage and leave "space" for the growing economies of the developing world.

* * *

The quality of people's lives depends largely on the physical, social and economic conditions of the villages, towns and cities in which they live. Today, some 2.5 billion people reside in urban areas. The number of urban dwellers is expected to grow rapidly in the years ahead, reaching 3 billion by the year 2000 and nearly 5 billion by 2025—an increase of almost 60 per cent. The environmental and developmental repercussions of this rapid, and often uncontrolled, urbanization could be profound: a breakdown in urban services, the spread of slums and social decline could well pose the most serious threats to human welfare and the environment in many countries.

Managing *human settlements* in a way that avoids these risks is an essential component of Agenda 21. This third theme of a *Habitable World* is central to ensuring a livable, healthy and sustainable environment for all through a qualitative improvement in human settlements services, such as better shelter, water supply, energy and transport, and the efficient handling of the problems of urban pollution, solid wastes and sewage.

Most urban municipal systems in developing countries find it difficult to keep pace with the need to provide safe water supplies, health care and job opportunities. Several fragile economies in the developing world are already burdened heavily by debt. They must deal with unfavourable terms of trade, a dependence on external supplies of food and energy, and inadequate institutional and professional capacities. The resulting environmental deterioration translates quickly into economic decline and human suffering.

In many urban areas, the general environment is exceedingly polluted and endangers the health of hundreds of millions of people. Many countries experience high levels of pollution in urban areas from energy production plants, industrial activities and transport systems that were put in place with little regard for environmental protection. While there have been notable improvements in most industrialized countries, this has not generally been the case in developing countries, where the deterioration of environmental conditions in urban fringe areas continues unabated. A priority in urban areas should be to clean up and maintain an environment that does not impair human health without, at the same time, impeding development.

Waste minimization has emerged at the top of the hierarchy of industrial and municipal waste management options that range from reduction at source to recycling and reuse to treatment and safe disposal. Waste minimization involves the elimination of waste generation through technological and managerial change. It is also part of a broader, preventive approach toward urban environmental management that includes pollution prevention and cleaner technology strategies.

Cities of the industrialized world are also centres of growing environmental pressures, such as air pollution, deteriorating infrastructure, homelessness, traffic congestion and tax and revenue sharing systems that are no longer equitable or viable.

But there also exist a number of positive examples where political will and a firm leadership and initiative have helped redevelop city centres, bringing a new balance between core areas and suburbs and revitalizing much of the quality of urban life.

* * *

The demands that people make on resources are in many cases unsustainable. These resources are already being depleted or degraded at a rapid rate. Changing consumption patterns to more efficient and responsible levels and reducing demographic pressures will help contain some of these demands. At the same time, it is essential that environmentally sounder ways of using resources be developed to meet society's needs. Renewable resources must be managed, not mined.

In the past, the Earth's natural resources and its capacity to assimilate waste were taken for granted. The unprecedented increase in human numbers and activities since the industrial revolution, particularly in this century, has given rise to a deterioration of the environment and depletion of natural resources that threaten the future of our planet. The carrying and absorptive capacity of the Earth's natural systems must be valued as an economic resource if sustainability for the present and future generations is to be assured.

Efficient resource use forms the basis of the fourth theme of a *Fertile World*. These action programmes focus on the urgency to reverse the destruction of renewable resources and implement strategies for the sustainable use of land, freshwater, biological and genetic resources and biotechnology. This must be done in a manner that raises productivity and meets the rising demand on agriculture and forests while ensuring the sustainable management of fragile ecosystems.

There are fragile—and important—ecosystems in deserts, semi-arid lands, mountains, wetlands, small islands and certain coastal areas possessing unique features and resources. Most of these ecosystems are regional in scope, as they transcend national boundaries. Other major ecosystems, such as mountains, are important sources of water, energy and biological diversity and provide minerals and forest and agricultural products as well as recreation. They also represent the complex and interrelated ecology of our planet. The central thrust of the Agenda 21 action programmes here is to incorporate the multisectoral nature of land, water, energy and biotic resource growth into socio-economic development and the multi-interest use of these resources for agriculture, forestry, industry, urban development, inland fisheries, transportation, recreation and other activities.

The core challenge of sustainable agriculture is to raise productivity and incomes, especially of the poor, without irreversibly degrading and depleting critical life-support systems such as soil and water. In this context, the issue of food security deserves special emphasis. Global, national and local food security strategies must ensure sufficient production and distribution of, and access to, affordable food. In many countries, agricultural practices have led to severe degradation and pollution of the resource base, especially in fragile ecosystems. The provision here of alternative livelihoods and sustainable practices deserves foremost attention.

Freshwater resources are an essential component of the Earth's hydrosphere and an indispensable part of all terrestrial ecosystems. With the growth in world population and the rapid increase in economic activities, demand for water has already outstripped supply in many regions, with competing demands leading to critical water management problems and creating, in some areas, a potential source of conflict. Water supply problems have been further exacerbated by increasing pollution. Water resource policies must form an integral part of the overall sustainable development policies that take into account the environmental and socio-economic constraints and objectives. There is a need for strategies to develop and flexibly allocate surface and groundwater resources in a manner that reflects existing and anticipated needs and opportunities.

Much of the world's energy is currently produced and consumed in ways that are unsustainable. The need to control atmospheric emissions of greenhouse and other gases and substances will be based, increasingly, on efficiency in energy production and use as well as on a growing reliance on environmentally sound and safe energy systems and technologies. Energy sources for sustainable development will need to be applied in ways that respect the atmosphere, human health and the environment as a whole.

Increasing attention is being given to the condition of the world's forests and to the role they play in local economies and in enhancing the quality of life. In the context of environmentally sound and sustainable development, the benefits to be derived from trees, forests and forest lands are wide and varied. Forests are not only sources of timber and firewood but also play an important role in soil conservation, the regulation of hydrological cycles, exchange of gases and nutrients, including carbon dioxide, and the maintenance of reservoirs of rich biodiversity. Many local populations have understood the multiple benefits for their livelihoods obtained from forests. It is only recently, however, that the fundamental value of forests has emerged on a wider national and global scale. The realization that forests significantly affect the lives of both local and distant populations and play a critical role in global environment and development issues has helped place forest-related issues on the national planning and international agendas. Of particular importance is the need for the international community to support the implementation of the non–legally binding Forest Principles, approved at the Rio Conference in June of 1992, on the management, conservation and sustainable development of all types of forests. Consideration should also be given to the need and feasibility of appropriate internationally agreed arrangements to promote international cooperation.

Biological diversity—or "biodiversity"—is one of the Earth's primary sources of natural capital. It plays a vital environmental and developmental role that is not accorded economic value, but is crucial to our future. Biological resources constitute a capital asset with great potential for yielding sustainable benefits. Their economic and social value is poorly appreciated and their true real value underestimated. Too often, only their short-term commercial market values are taken into account. While it is difficult to quantify the values of some aspects of biodiversity, much can nevertheless be done to value commercially harvested products such as timber, fish and medicinal plants. Biodiversity's potential contributions to human health and welfare, through the derivation of new and improved food crops, the development of pharmaceutical products and the improvement of biotechnological processes, cannot be overestimated. Urgent measures are required to arrest current trends of increasing species loss and declining global biodiversity. International cooperation is essential, especially since most of the world's biodiversity exists in the developing world, while the technological and financial capacity to conserve and develop genetic resources exists in the developed world.

Biotechnology has wide application in several sectors of great economic relevance for both developing and developed countries. New biotechnological techniques, used in conjunction with traditional methods, can substantially multiply the values available from the sustainable development of biological resources. Sophisticated biotechnological tools and products now being developed offer an impressive array of possible applications for national development. These should be widely available to all countries to help build their national capacities, increase food, feed and fibre production and enhance the overall quality of life. There is a need to elaborate integrated programmes which use biotechnology to ensure development, while providing adequate mechanisms for germplasm conservation and utilization and ensuring conditions which are safe for human health and the environment.

* * *

An important component of the scheme for resource management consists of programmes and institutional arrangements to make certain that assets outside national boundaries are fairly and responsibly used. Regional and global conventions for this purpose should be supported by practical programmes to effect them.

The fifth theme of *global and regional resources* comprises action strategies to deal with the atmosphere, oceans, seas and living marine resources. Global climate and weather, hydrological and carbon cycles and several physical processes on land are heavily influenced by both oceanic and atmospheric processes. The Earth's capacity to sustain and nourish life depends primarily on the quality and composition of its atmosphere. Human activities have reached a point where they are now altering the balancing systems of the atmosphere, which make life possible on Earth. Environmental problems on a global and regional scale, such as the depletion of the ozone layer, desertification, climate change, acid rain, and air, water and marine contamination, threaten the future habitability of our planet. This is a set of complex problems: human activity affects climate in ways that are complicated and multifaceted, involving time horizons that separate cause and effect which go well beyond the accustomed time-scales of political and economic decision-making. Nevertheless, the risks are clearly of critical, perhaps decisive, importance to our collective future and require the firm application of the precautionary principle.

Efforts to protect the atmosphere can be enhanced by using materials and resources efficiently in all industries; improving technologies for pollution abatement; replacing chlorofluorocarbons (CFCs) and other ozone-depleting substances with appropriate substitutes, consistent with the 1987 Montreal Protocol; and scaling down industrial by-products and waste. Compliance with control measures within the

Montreal Protocol and its 1990 amendments will assist in *preventing stratospheric ozone depletion*. To tackle the problem of climate change in a comprehensive and equitable manner, the international community endorsed a legally binding treaty, the United Nations Framework Convention on Climate Change, in Rio de Janeiro in June of 1992. Signed by 153 Member States of the United Nations as well as the European Economic Community, the Convention aims to stabilize greenhouse gas concentrations in the atmosphere at a level that would prevent dangerous anthropogenic interference with the climate system.

The world's oceans play an influential role in the biogeochemical processes of the planet on a local, regional and global scale. Energy, climate and weather, the hydrological and carbon cycles, and atmospheric and physical processes worldwide are all critically influenced by the properties of oceanic processes.

The oceans are also a vast fount of living and non-living resources. The increase in marine catches over the past two decades is largely the result of new fishing technologies. Some of these methods have precipitated the decline of several marine, bird, reptile and mammal populations. Seals and large whale species have been overexploited, some to the brink of extinction. One cause of this is their common property status which could, in the absence of appropriate management regimes, lead to the depletion of stocks. This status encourages poor practices such as habitat destruction, the use of illegal techniques such as dynamite and chemicals, or intensive dredging, seining, driftnetting and trawling, incidental capture of non-target species and unselective fishing.

The physical and ecological degradation of coastal areas is also hastening. The principal cause of coastal management problems lies in the growth of human populations and their economic activities. The rapid development of coastal settlements and the expansion of recreational areas and centres of maritime transport, coupled with the concentration of industrial development along coasts, have resulted in quickening coastal degradation.

Marine pollution can be observed from the poles to the tropics and from beaches to abyssal depths. Apart from ocean waste dumping, a wide range of activities on land also contributes to the release of contaminants, either directly or through rivers and the atmosphere. Present seaborne activities have only a minor impact: 40 per cent of the contaminants arrive by rivers and 30 per cent through the atmosphere. Maritime and dumping activities contribute some 10 per cent each. The last few decades have seen a precipitous rise in coastal pollution and the destruction of coastal marine habitats, with a corresponding decline in many areas in the overall catch of marine fish species through overfishing and marine pollution.

Agenda 21 gives special emphasis to the need for a global partnership to augment our understanding of these phenomena and for internationally binding agreements to protect these atmospheric and oceanic resources in a common and *Shared World*.

* * *

Production processes and resource use necessarily generate waste. The rise in production—with continuing patterns of wasteful and destructive consumption around the world—could well overwhelm economic development at local, national and global levels by the waste and pollution it produces. There has been an increase in the amount of residues that are not being reintegrated into the ecosystems, causing considerable problems for human health and environmental quality.

The volume and complexity of waste generation and its composition have also changed substantially over the years.

The use of chemicals is essential to the development process and to the promotion of human well-being. They are extensively used by all societies, irrespective of their stage of development. Chemicals can, however, take a heavy toll on human health and harm the environment. It would be prudent, therefore, to learn the properties of chemicals and take appropriate precautionary measures in regard to their safe handling, use and final disposal.

Inadequate waste disposal affects national wealth and productivity in many ways. The repercussions on human health are perhaps the most significant. Over 80 per cent of all diseases and over one third of deaths in developing countries are caused by the ingestion of waste-contaminated food and water. It has been estimated that as much as one tenth of a person's productive life in developing societies is sacrificed to waste-related diseases. The economic burden of the resulting expenses in curative medicine and loss of productivity has significant consequences for overall national development. This is not to mention the costs in terms of human misery and lowered quality of life that affects millions around the globe, especially the poor.

Reducing waste generation, recycling wastes productively, finding safe means for waste disposal and dealing with the illegal trade in hazardous wastes: these are essential steps in *managing chemicals and wastes* in a healthy and habitable *Clean World.*

* * *

These six motifs of Agenda 21 are the predominant themes upon which are based the substantive action programmes to foster the sustainable use of natural resources for human development and ensure equitable living standards and quality of life for all in a clean and sustaining environment. An essential element for success and the early realization of these goals is the full and active participation of all relevant social groups—women, youth, indigenous people and their communities, non-governmental organizations, farmers, local authorities, trade unions, businessmen, industrialists and scientists. The diverse backgrounds, skills and experiences that these groups bring to the fore are essential to effect the transition to sustainable growth. The genuine commitment and depth of this broad public participation in all aspects of decision-making will be critical to the effective implementation of the objectives, policies and mechanisms in all the programme areas of Agenda 21.

People's participation and responsibility form the basis of the final theme of a *People's World* in Agenda 21. Strengthening the role of major groups to achieve sustainable development would involve a massive increase in education, public awareness and training. It will, in addition, require greater transparency and accountability in governmental decision-making processes. All of these participatory programmes are aimed at placing issues of environment and development at the heart of decision-making at all levels and ensuring the maximum participation and contribution of all groups of society.

* * *

In order to implement Agenda 21, a variety of *essential means* must be made available to all nations. The integration of environment and development must be reflected in a reorientation of attitudes, in changes in decision-making and in the *data and information systems* for planning, implementation and monitoring. The availability of accurate and timely information to decision makers and the general public is an essential element of the effort towards sustainable development.

Agenda 21 puts forward actions for the collection, processing and dissemination of data and information relevant to each of the sectoral and cross-sectoral issues.

The developing world has far less access than industrialized countries to the information it needs to make informed choices and decisions about the environment and economic activities. This gap is widening. Many developing countries lack sufficient capacity to collect, assess and disseminate data. Widely used economic indicators, such as gross national product, do not reflect the environmental sustainability of development processes. To ensure that planning is based on reliable and relevant information, a number of measures are proposed in Agenda 21 to strengthen data collection for sustainable development.

The ability of a country to make the transition to sustainable development depends to a large extent on its endogenous institutional and professional capacity. Strengthening these national capacities is a core element of all Agenda 21 programmes. National capacity-building represents a challenge to both developing and industrialized countries alike, requiring long-term commitments and accountability on the part of all Governments, donor institutions and programmes. The industrialized countries would have to implement their own sustainable development programmes and strengthen their efforts—whether bilateral or multilateral—to support capacity-building in developing countries. Much support for capacity-building can be provided through cooperation at the regional and subregional levels.

A country-driven participatory process and a sustained commitment to building endogenous human, technological and institutional capacity are indispensable prerequisites to break out of the present, deeply entrenched patterns of environmental and economic deterioration, dependency and vulnerability. Developing countries should establish their own priorities for sustainable development, to be implemented through a coalition of both domestic and international resources. Reinforcing national capacity would enable a demand-oriented approach rather than a supply-driven process, where developing countries coordinate the relevant international and regional technical cooperation for their transition to, and achievement of, sustainable development.

Strengthening the endogenous national capacities of developing countries is, therefore, a principal priority of Agenda 21 and includes support for their institutional and normative framework for environmental policy formulation and management. These countries should also evolve greater capacities to assimilate appropriate technologies and engage in global cross-flows of relevant knowledge and information. This calls for sustained domestic commitments on the part of developing countries, as well as for new levels of international commitment and support.

Environmentally sound technologies are fundamental for the transition to sustainable development. Ever since the industrial revolution, development has been energy- and resource-consumptive, as well as polluting, to an unsustainable degree. The Earth's natural systems can provide neither infinite natural resources nor an endless capacity to assimilate wastes. Consequently, pollution abatement and recycling technologies are essential ingredients of sustainable development.

The global need for environmentally sound technology extends to sectors and requires a much greater international effort in scientific cooperation and technology transfer. The related programmes of Agenda 21 deal with issues of *science for sustainable development* and *environmentally sound technology* as they apply to sustainable development. The developed countries have, over time, built up a substantial base of scientific and technological knowledge that should be shared with the developing world to ensure a rapid transition to environmentally sound and sustainable development. In particular, the modalities of the access to this technology on favourable terms, including preferential and concessional terms, will be important to the early and widespread achievement of the goals of sustainable development at national, regional and global levels. At the same time, the indigenous knowledge and cultural heritage of developing countries must be integrated with modern knowledge and technology to ensure a viable transition to more sustainable lifestyles and responsible use of the Earth's resources.

With well over 100 existing *international legal agreements and instruments* dealing with environmental matters, Governments find it increasingly difficult to keep pace with the international regulatory process and implement it nationally. At the same time, world-wide coverage, participation and compliance have become increasingly important to sustainable development and environmental security. The special needs and concerns of developing countries in this respect, often inadequately covered in the past, require priority attention.

To translate the achievements of the Rio Conference into practical action, *international institutional arrangements* have to be set in place for the implementation of issues of environment and development at the national, subregional, regional and international levels.

The nucleus of international cooperation and intergovernmental decision-making for the integration of environment and development issues and the review and monitoring of Agenda 21 at the national, regional and international levels will be a high-level Commission on Sustainable Development, set up in accordance with Article 68 of the Charter of the United Nations. The focal point for inter-agency coordination within the United Nations system would be the Secretary-General, in his capacity as head of the inter-agency Administrative Committee on Coordination (ACC). Critical to the successful implementation of Agenda 21 will be the roles played by the relevant United Nations agencies and organizations, such as the United Nations Environment Programme, the United Nations Development Programme, the United Nations Conference on Trade and Development and the United Nations Sudano-Sahelian Office, as well as regional and subregional programmes such as the regional development banks.

The provision of financial resources and technology is essential for developing countries to meet the goals embodied in Agenda 21. It is important to note here that the non-availability of financial resources would make it impossible to implement the programmes in Agenda 21 and would void them of any significance. Also, the cost of inaction would far outweigh the costs of implementing Agenda 21 and narrow the choices of future generations as well.

The secretariat of the United Nations Conference on Environment and Development has estimated that the average annual costs (1993-2000) of implementing Agenda 21 in the developing countries will be over $600 billion, including about $125 billion on grant or concessional terms from the international community. These are indicative and order-of-magnitude estimates only. Actual costs will depend upon the specific strategies and programmes Governments decide upon for implementation.

Official Development Assistance (ODA) will be the main source of external funding to implement Agenda 21. Developed countries at the Rio Conference reaffirmed their commitments to reach the accepted United Nations target of 0.7 per cent of gross national product for ODA, and agreed to augment their aid programmes to reach that target as soon as possible and ensure the prompt implementation of Agenda 21. Progress towards this target will be monitored by the new Commission on Sustainable Development.

The financing of the implementation of Agenda 21— which reflects a global consensus integrating environmental considerations into an accelerated development process—will also require a substantial flow of *new and additional financial resources* to developing countries to enable them to achieve sustainable growth and participate fully in international environmental cooperation. All available funding mechanisms and sources will be used, including the International Development Association (IDA) and the restructured Global Environmental Facility (GEF).

Agenda 21 is a realistic action programme to chart a new course for the sustainable future of the human family. It seeks to ensure that, within the lifetime of someone born today, the world will have edged ever closer toward justice, security and prosperity for all. Agenda 21 includes concrete measures and incentives to reduce the negative environmental impacts of the rich, to quicken the pace of growth in developing countries, to eliminate their pervasive poverty and reduce unsustainable rates of population growth that menace their development as well as their environment. It is based on the premise that sustainable development is not just an option but an imperative, in both environmental and developmental terms, and that while the transition to sustainable development will be difficult, it is entirely feasible. It is a call for a fundamental shift in priorities for Governments and people, a complete integration of environmental aspects into economic and sectoral policy and decision-making in every sphere of activity, and a major redeployment of human and financial resources at the national and international levels.

III

Agenda 21:
The Priority Actions

AGENDA 21:
THE PRIORITY ACTIONS

HUMANITY stands at a defining moment in history. The world is confronted with abiding disparities within and between nations, a deepening of hunger, poverty, illiteracy and ill health. The ecological and economic repercussions of ozone depletion, climate change, soil and forest degradation, decline of biological diversity and expanding pollution of land, water and air augur badly for the future of our small planet.

Agenda 21 is a bold mandate for change. It is a blueprint for partnership on a global scale to meet the challenges of the 1990s and the 21st century, a basis for urgent action by the international community to integrate environment and development and secure our common and sustainable future.

Agenda 21 is a call to modify the norms of our economic behaviour, based on a new awareness of the destructive impact of human activity on the environment. It includes concrete and realistic measures and incentives to reduce the negative environmental impacts of the industrialized nations, encourage rapid, sustained and equitable economic growth in the developing countries, eliminate their pervasive poverty and lower the unsustainable rates of population growth that menace the environment of the poor as well as their development. Agenda

21 calls for a major shift in the priorities of Governments and people to fully integrate the environmental dimension with economic and sectoral policies and decision-making in every sphere of economic and environmental activity, and redeploy human and financial resources at both national and international levels.

The action programmes of Agenda 21 are arranged around principal substantive social themes, such as the *Revitalization of Growth with Sustainability*, *Sustainable Living* for all and *Human Settlements* development. These would promote *Efficient Resource Use*, *Global and Regional Resources, and Managing Chemicals and Wastes*, through a wide and responsible public participation at the local, national, regional and global levels.

1

REVITALIZING GROWTH WITH SUSTAINABILITY

FINANCIAL, trade and governmental systems have made unprecedented contributions to global economic growth this century. At the same time, their insufficient consideration of environmental and socio-economic realities have led to conditions that threaten development and human progress. The international economic system has, over the years, favoured the excessive exploitation of raw materials, in developing countries in particular, and often at serious environmental cost. The same system has also rendered the fragile economies of the developing countries highly vulnerable to changes in world economic conditions, over which they have only nominal control. In recent years, and largely as a result of debt-servicing imperatives, there has been a negative net transfer of finances from the industrialized to the developing world, leaving the latter with few resources to combat poverty and environmental degradation.

These debilitating patterns are indicative of the need to integrate environmental and developmental considerations throughout the decision-making process at all levels and in all sectors, including international economic relations. It is critical that these international relations are environmentally responsible and equitable, particularly with regard to financial flows, trade, transnational investment and access to science and technology.

Revitalizing growth with sustainability

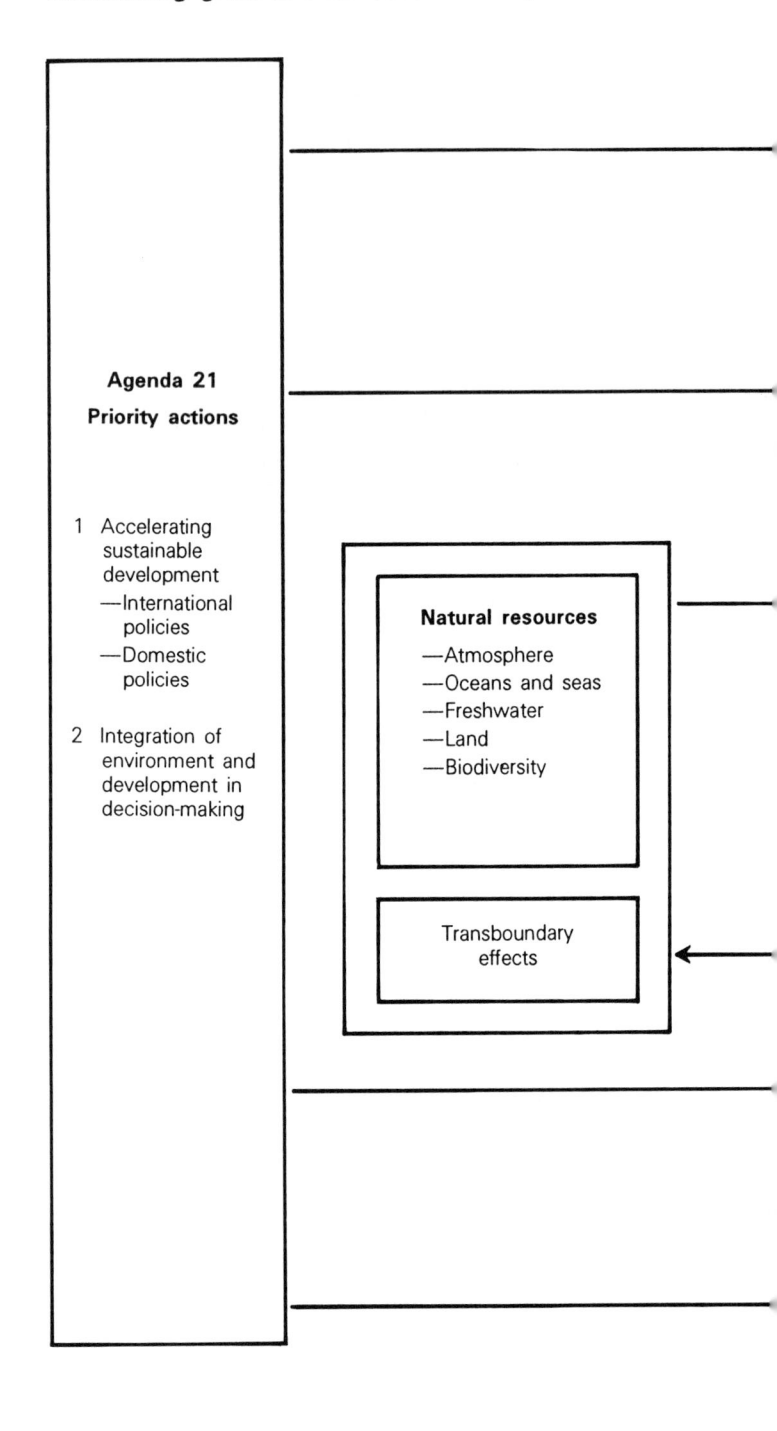

**Agenda 21
Priority actions**

1 Accelerating
  sustainable
  development
  —International
   policies
  —Domestic
   policies

2 Integration of
  environment and
  development in
  decision-making

Natural resources

—Atmosphere
—Oceans and seas
—Freshwater
—Land
—Biodiversity

Transboundary
effects

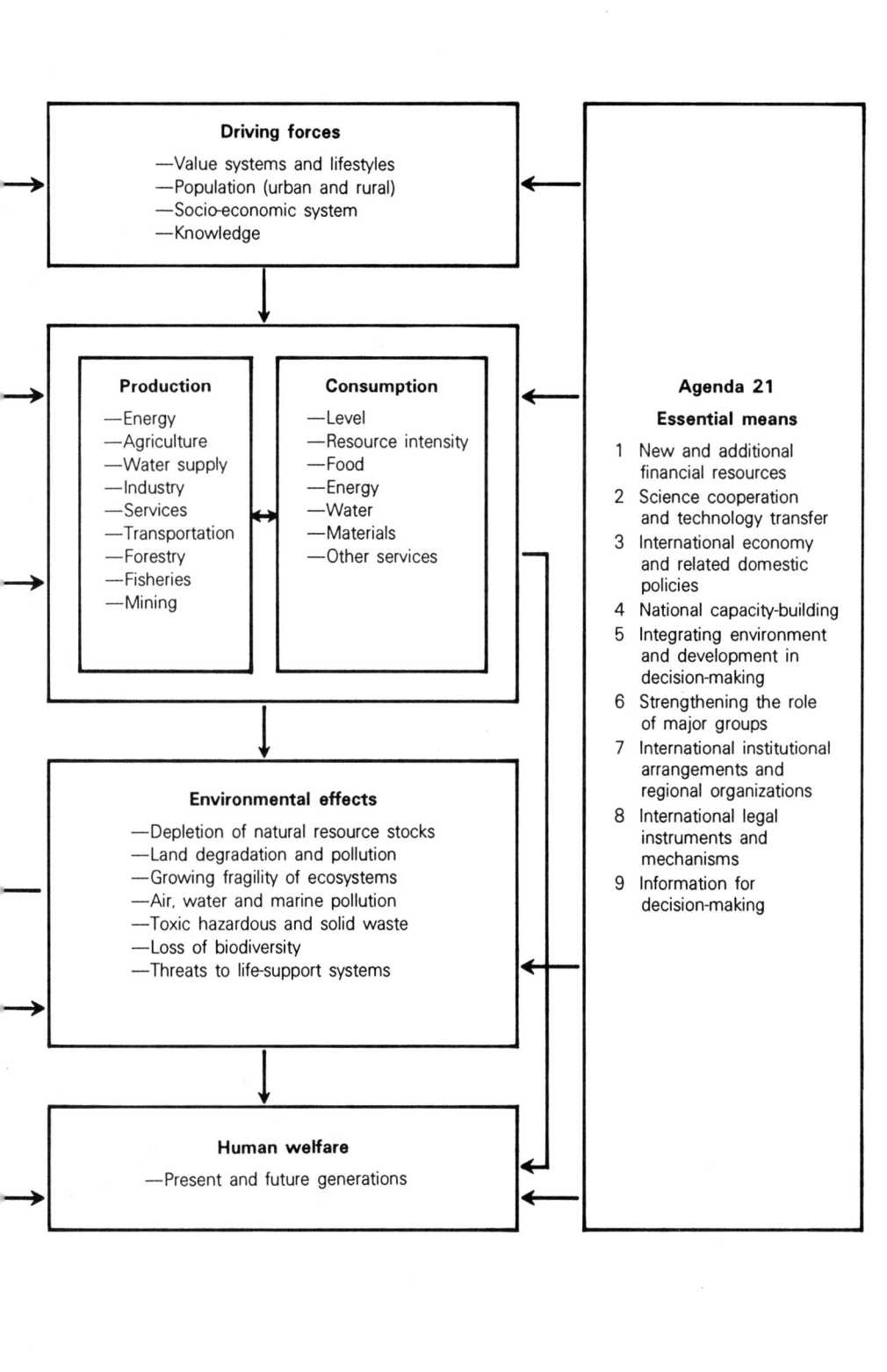

Driving forces
—Value systems and lifestyles
—Population (urban and rural)
—Socio-economic system
—Knowledge

Production
—Energy
—Agriculture
—Water supply
—Industry
—Services
—Transportation
—Forestry
—Fisheries
—Mining

Consumption
—Level
—Resource intensity
—Food
—Energy
—Water
—Materials
—Other services

Agenda 21
Essential means
1 New and additional financial resources
2 Science cooperation and technology transfer
3 International economy and related domestic policies
4 National capacity-building
5 Integrating environment and development in decision-making
6 Strengthening the role of major groups
7 International institutional arrangements and regional organizations
8 International legal instruments and mechanisms
9 Information for decision-making

Environmental effects
—Depletion of natural resource stocks
—Land degradation and pollution
—Growing fragility of ecosystems
—Air, water and marine pollution
—Toxic hazardous and solid waste
—Loss of biodiversity
—Threats to life-support systems

Human welfare
—Present and future generations

Revitalizing growth with sustainability

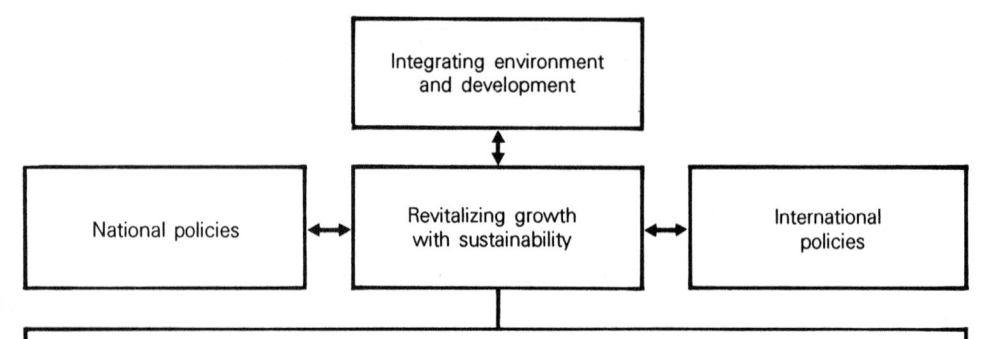

```
              Integrating environment
                 and development
                         ↕
National policies ↔ Revitalizing growth ↔ International
                     with sustainability    policies
```

Cross-sectoral linkages

Combating poverty: Providing sustainable livelihoods (ch. 2.1)

Changing consumption patterns: Less wasteful lifestyles; sustainable consumption levels; informed consumer choices (ch. 2.2)

Demographic dynamics and sustainability: Global challenges; national and local level integration of population and environment (ch. 2.3)

Health: Pollution health risks; urban health; basic needs; communicable diseases; vulnerable groups (ch. 2.4)

Human settlements: Shelter; land and settlement management; environmental infrastructure; energy and transport; human resources and capacity-building; disaster-prone areas (ch. 3.1)

Urban water supplies: Drinking water; sanitation; intersectoral planning; monitoring (ch. 3.2)

Solid waste management: Waste minimization; safe disposal; expansion of services; recycling (ch. 3.3)

Urban pollution and health: Air pollution; municipal health planning; radiation protection (ch. 3.4)

Land resources: Integrated planning and management (ch. 4.1)

Freshwater resources: Integrated assessment, development and management; protection of quality and resources; drinking water; sanitation; water for agriculture (ch. 4.2)

Sustainable agriculture and rural development: Policy, planning and programming; human resources participation; land use; conservation and rehabilitation; freshwater; plant and animal genetic resources; pest management; plant nutrition; rural energy; rural employment; food security (ch. 4.3)

Combating deforestation: Multiple utilization of trees, forests and lands; assessment and monitoring; international and regional cooperation (ch. 4.4)

Managing fragile ecosystems
4.5.1 Combating desertification and drought
Information and monitoring; afforestation and reforestation; alternative livelihoods; anti-desertification programmes and action plans; drought preparedness and relief
4.5.2 Sustainable mountain development
Information; integrated watershed development; alternative livelihoods

Biological diversity: Information; benefits and use; conservation; capacity-building (ch. 4.6)

Environmentally sound management of biotechnology: Productivity of food and feed; health; environment protection; safety enabling mechanisms; international cooperation (ch. 4.7)

Atmosphere: Sustainable energy development and consumption; transport systems; industry; agriculture; ozone depletion; addressing uncertainties (ch. 5.1)

Oceans and seas: Coastal area development; marine protection; living resources; uncertainties and climate change; international cooperation and coordination; island development (ch. 5.2)

Toxic chemicals: Chemical risks assessment; classification and labelling; information; risks management programmes (ch. 6.1)

Hazardous wastes: Cleaner production, waste minimization, institutional capacities; international cooperation for transboundary movement (ch. 6.2)

Radioactive wastes: International agreements for safe management (ch. 6.3)

Education, public awareness and training (ch. 7.1)

Strengthening the role of major groups: Women; youth; indigenous people and their communities; NGOs; farmers; local authorities; trade unions; business and industry; scientific and technological community (ch. 7.2)

The transition to sustainable development requires a more efficient use of resources, as well as the accountability for environmental and economic impacts of such use. More realistic economic values will have to be placed on the environment and our natural resources. The operation of market forces can be a powerful ally in providing the incentives to change. Nevertheless, economic growth in developing countries is essential for sustainable development and cannot be overly constrained. Policies that control trade and the flow of global finances have a major impact on sustainable development. Agricultural and other commodities, the most important income sources for developing countries, are also among the products most protected by the trade policies of developed countries. The international trading system should reduce tariffs and phase out non-tariff barriers to trade.

The economic valuation of natural resources on the basis of the monetary costs of extraction and distribution has often resulted in inadequate incentives for sustainable resource use and, in turn, overconsumption of resource-based products and environmental degradation. The internalization of all environmental costs is an important measure, not only in regard to trade and consumption patterns, but also to resources such as oceans, freshwater and forests.

The transition to revitalized growth with sustainability will necessitate the innovative formulation and use of pricing policies, economic instruments, access to international markets and assistance and a range of regulatory measures. The urgent need to accelerate sustainable development calls for a universal partnership to ensure that new international and national policies bring about fundamental changes in the integration and accounting of environment and development in decision-making.

1.1 INTERNATIONAL COOPERATION TO ACCELERATE SUSTAINABLE DEVELOPMENT IN DEVELOPING COUNTRIES AND RELATED DOMESTIC POLICIES

International economic relations, such as trade and financial flows, have a significant influence on the ability of developing countries to achieve economic growth in a manner consistent with the sound management of natural resources.

World trade today is of the order of $6 trillion, the greater part of which is accounted for by the industrialized economies. The conditions governing international trade are of particular importance to the developing world, since trade plays a crucial role in their drive for structural transformation and growth.

The commodity sector dominates the economies of many developing countries in terms of production, employment and export earnings. The deterioration of terms of trade affecting developing countries, and protectionist barriers limiting exports to developed country markets, impair the ability of developing countries to mobilize, through international trade, the resources needed to fund investments required for sustainable development. Agricultural subsidies, high tariffs and tariff escalation on processed products are particular obstacles to developing country export trade. As the trade system provides for the exchange of goods and services and can modify patterns of production and consumption, it may have both a positive and negative impact on the environment. An open trading and financial system, which distributes global production in accordance with comparative advantage, would be beneficial to all trading partners.

International trade can, in some cases, provide the additional resources needed for economic growth and development, while also enabling significant investment to improve environmental quality. In most cases, however, the mobilization of domestic resources should be the main component of national investment. A sound environment can, in turn, provide the resources needed to sustain growth and underpin a continuing expansion of national and international resource use.

The financial resources for investment are critical for the ability of developing countries to achieve the economic growth needed to improve the welfare of their populations and to meet their basic needs in a sustainable manner, all without deteriorating or depleting the resource base that underpins development. Sustainable development requires increased investment, for which financial resources are needed. Many developing countries have experienced a decade-long situation of negative net transfer of financial resources, during which the payments they had to make, in particular for debt-servicing, exceeded their financial receipts. As a result, domestically mobilized resources had to be transferred abroad instead of being invested locally for sustainable economic development. The debt crisis continues to impair the functioning of the international financial system and prevents it from fulfilling its vital role in providing funds to support development and trade. This unfavourable external environment facing developing countries makes domestic resource mobilization and efficient allocation and utilization of domestically mobilized resources all the more important in order to promote sustainable development.

To meet this challenge, the international community should promote an open international trading system that improves developing country access to international markets. This will likely require the integration of commodity prices to include environmental costs. The removal of existing distortions in international trade is essential. This needs substantial and progressive reductions in the support and protection of agriculture—internal regimes, market access and export subsidies—as well as industry and other sectors. Trade liberalization should be pursued across economic sectors to enable it to contribute to sustainable development.

Developing countries should develop domestic policies which maximize the benefits of trade liberalization. In particular, they should remove biases against exports and discourage inefficient import-substitution, promote infrastructure required to improve the efficiency of export and import trade, expand processing, improve marketing practices and reduce dependence on primary commodity exports. The operation of international commodity agreements and arrangements, compensation mechanisms for shortfalls in commodity export earnings and better marketing techniques are also important in improving the situation of developing countries.

To facilitate this process, an international trade/environmental consultative and dispute settlements process should be developed to ensure that environment-related standards are not used as non-tariff barriers to trade. This should take account of special factors affecting environmental and trade policies in developing countries and promote multilateral agreements rather than unilateral action.

In regard to finance, it is necessary to ensure substantial positive net resource flows to developing countries by increasing the official development assistance to internationally envisaged targets and substantially to reduce debts and debt-servicing. The continued clearing of outstanding balances would restore the ability of the international financial system to contribute to growth and development. At the same time, extended coordinated action could substantially reduce debt owed to private banks and official bilateral creditors. Debt owed to bilateral official creditors by low income debtors should continue to be written off.

In a number of countries, policies are necessary to correct misdirected public spending, large budget deficits and other macroeconomic imbalances, restrictive policies and distortions in the areas of exchange rates, investment and finance and obstacles to entrepreneurship. In industrialized countries, such policy reforms would help release resources to support the transition to sustainable development domestically and among developing countries. An increase in domestic savings in developed countries would be a complement to policies to restrain consumption on environmental grounds.

1.2 INTEGRATING ENVIRONMENT AND DEVELOPMENT IN DECISION-MAKING

Economic development has received the world's major attention. During the last two decades, however, there has been increasing concern about its adverse effects on the environment. To redress this, environmental policies have been formulated and implemented, but have rarely been integrated with economic policies. It is now clear that sustainable development requires the integration of environmental and socio-economic factors.

In order to make the transition to sustainability, Governments are urged to assist in *integrating environment and development at the policy, planning and management levels*. This will require a fundamental change in the way decisions are made and, more importantly, in the perceptions and attitudes underlying the development process. The decision-making process will have to be restructured to integrate economic and environmental issues comprehensively, making the attainment of sustainability an explicit societal goal. Sustainable macro-economic management for socially responsible, efficient and environmentally sound development must be placed at the centre of the development agenda. All sectors of society must participate and contribute to the shaping of this new agenda.

Policies would have to be designed to foster changes in the way the environment is perceived in relation to the economy and the provision of goods and services. Policies should promote more appropriate production and consumption patterns, as well as shifts in technology use and macro- and micro-economic management, that anticipate and prevent the depletion of resources and irreversible environmental degradation. These new policies would facilitate the shift from a *post facto* approach to an anticipatory approach in addressing environmental degradation and depletion at their roots.

Modifications in decision-making and governmental institutional structures, already started in some countries, have highlighted the need for systematic consideration of critical environmental issues when decisions are made on economic, fiscal, sectoral, trade and other policies. To translate policies into effective action, it would be necessary to build and develop stronger institutional structures and capacities and to coordinate actions more fully, so that they all contribute to the goal of sustainability and the satisfaction of human needs. Coordination and consultation mechanisms will have to harmonize policies and full cross-sectoral coordination and cooperation will also have to be achieved. New forms of dialogue would be important to link the various institutions and social actors—industry, science, environmental groups and the public—with the process of developing effective approaches towards development and the environment.

Development should be planned and managed in an integrative and adaptive manner and should operate from as solid and up-to-date an information base as possible. To this end, the use of social, economic and environmental data and information in planning and management should be improved. Moreover, widely-used indicators of economic performance should be adjusted to account for the crucial role the environment plays as a source of natural capital and as a sink for waste by-products generated during production processes. Governments should assist in *establishing systems for integrated environmental accounting*, in which the adjusted gross national product figures would provide economic policy makers with more accurate signals on national economic performance. Analyses should stress interactions and synergisms, and include analytical procedures assessing the environmental and developmental impacts. The status of development should be systematically monitored, and should include regular reviews of the state of human development, economic conditions and trends, the state of the environment and natural resources, as well as annual sustainable development reviews and accountability in various sectors and government departments. All relevant information should be widely disseminated, especially to the public.

Providing an effective legal and regulatory framework at the international, national and local levels is essential to transform environment and development policies into action. Most international agreements on environment and development require the enactment and enforcement of specific laws and regulations locally and nationally. The legal process, however, is often ill-adapted to the scale and pace of economic and social change. Developing countries stand in particular need of technical support in the drafting and practical application of new and revised legal instruments. Legal and regulatory instruments should be made more effective through regular reviews and assessments and the provision of adequate resources for effective implementation. Intergovernmental and non-governmental organizations should cooperate to provide Governments, especially in developing countries, with an integrated programme of environment and development law services, carefully adapted to the specific requirements of the recipient country's legal and administrative systems. The experience of several international agreements indicates both a low degree of compliance with reporting requirements and inadequate follow-up evaluation, owing in part to staff constraints in the countries concerned. Legal training in environment and development should, therefore, be strengthened. To develop improved and more harmonized compliance procedures, sample surveys should be undertaken that compare actual legislative and regulatory enactments with domestic follow-up actions.

Prices, markets and the rewards and penalties inherent in fiscal and economic policies also play powerful roles in moulding attitudes and behaviour towards the environment. In many countries the increasing use of market-oriented approaches, such as the "polluter pays" principle, has created cost-effective solutions, provided an important source of funds, promoted technological innovations and influenced environmental behaviour. As part of a general transition toward sustainable policies, Governments should help in *making effective use of economic instruments and market and other incentives* through, for example, the internalization of environmental costs to dispel the assumption that the environment is a free good. Governments should review policies and build on market-oriented approaches, removing subsidies and promoting new markets in the areas of pollution control and resource management. The use of pricing policies, taxation and market-oriented incentives should be explored as effective ways of addressing environment issues.

2

SUSTAINABLE LIVING

THE nations of the world have begun to realize that the Earth's carrying capacity is finite, and that global consumption, production and demographic patterns will have to be made sustainable if future generations are to live healthy, prosperous and satisfying lives. Achieving sustainable living for all requires an environmentally responsible global approach to modify these unsustainable patterns, involving efficiency and waste minimization changes in production processes, less wasteful consumption, reducing demographic pressures and ensuring access to health care.

More than 1 billion people on our planet are poor, malnourished and diseased—a certain indication of today's disparate and unsustainable patterns of production and consumption. Over 800 million people go hungry each day. Many among these are children. Nearly one and a half billion people are denied access to primary health care and are threatened by a host of diseases, most of which are easily avoidable. In light of present demographic pressures, meeting the needs of all the world's inhabitants will be an ever greater challenge. Alleviating poverty is a moral imperative and a *sine qua non* when addressing issues of sustainable development.

This century has seen a massive increase in the world's production and consumption, particularly in developed countries. Although stimulating economic growth in the short term, Governments now recognize that this globally unsustainable use of the Earth's resources has degraded the environment and generated unmanageable amounts of waste and pollution.

Natural resources and living standards are often the casualties of population growth. The impact of population on environment and development issues should be further analyzed. Human vulnerability in sensitive areas should be determined. It is proposed that population factors be thoroughly researched and incorporated into national planning, policy and decision-making.

Providing primary health care to everyone is a key aspect of alleviating poverty. Standards of health care, for those who receive indifferent or middling services, and specialized health care for environmentally related problems should be increased. Access to affordable health care, and facilities that communities can maintain on their own, are important factors.

In the decade of the 1990s, it is important that the world community make a social transition to poverty alleviation and sustainable consumption patterns. A world where poverty is endemic would always be susceptible to ecological and human crises. An improvement in living standards and development progress would also contribute toward the demographic transition to stable populations. Global cooperation and a vigorous and mutually beneficial partnership are essential to achieving the fundamental goal of improving human welfare throughout the world.

2.1 COMBATING POVERTY

Of the nearly 4.2 billion people in the developing world, some 25 per cent live in conditions of crippling poverty, without adequate food, basic education and health care, and deprived,

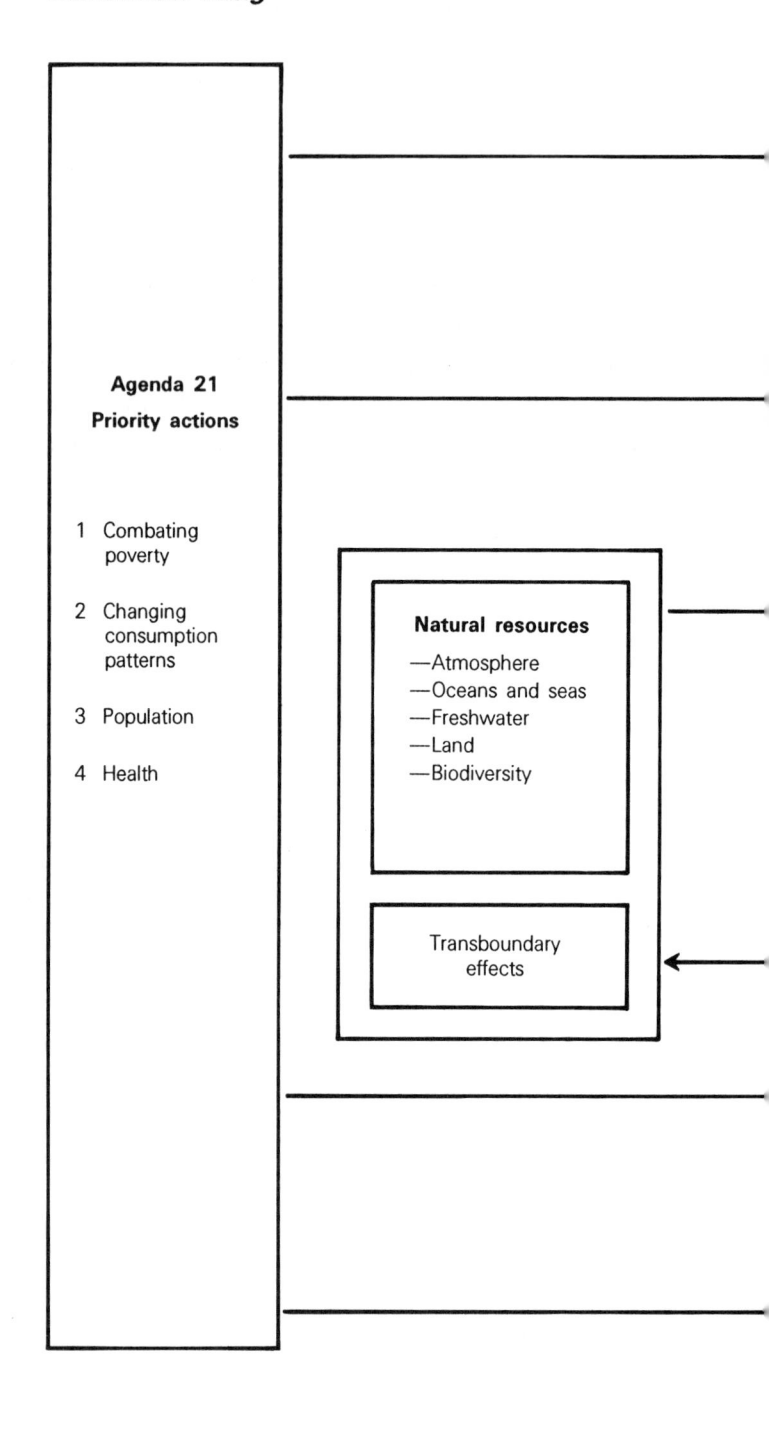

Sustainable living

**Agenda 21
Priority actions**

1 Combating poverty

2 Changing consumption patterns

3 Population

4 Health

Natural resources
—Atmosphere
—Oceans and seas
—Freshwater
—Land
—Biodiversity

Transboundary effects

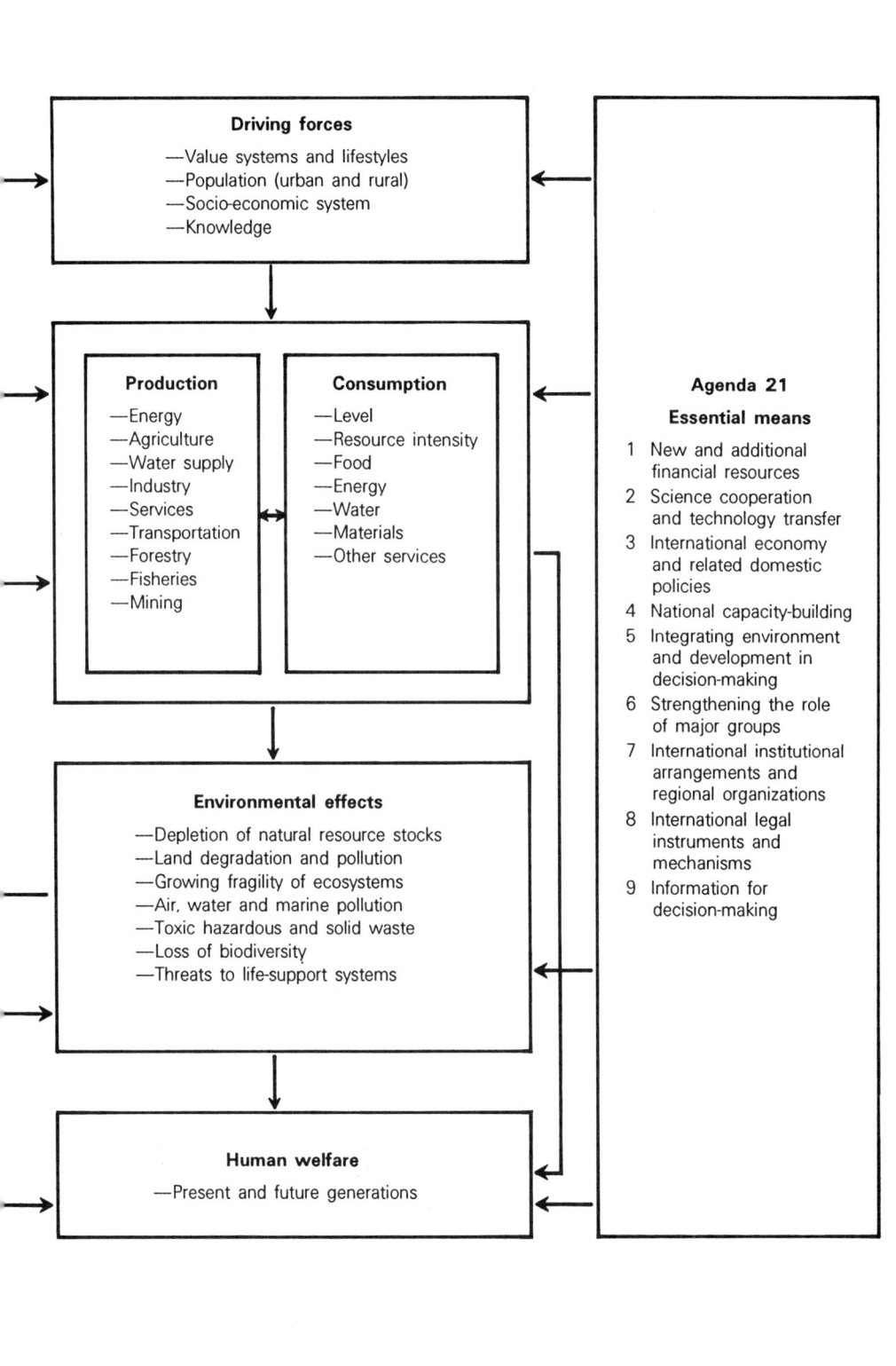

```
Driving forces
—Value systems and lifestyles
—Population (urban and rural)
—Socio-economic system
—Knowledge
```

```
Production                Consumption
—Energy                   —Level
—Agriculture              —Resource intensity
—Water supply             —Food
—Industry                 —Energy
—Services                 —Water
—Transportation           —Materials
—Forestry                 —Other services
—Fisheries
—Mining
```

```
Environmental effects
—Depletion of natural resource stocks
—Land degradation and pollution
—Growing fragility of ecosystems
—Air, water and marine pollution
—Toxic hazardous and solid waste
—Loss of biodiversity
—Threats to life-support systems
```

```
Human welfare
—Present and future generations
```

Agenda 21
Essential means

1. New and additional financial resources
2. Science cooperation and technology transfer
3. International economy and related domestic policies
4. National capacity-building
5. Integrating environment and development in decision-making
6. Strengthening the role of major groups
7. International institutional arrangements and regional organizations
8. International legal instruments and mechanisms
9. Information for decision-making

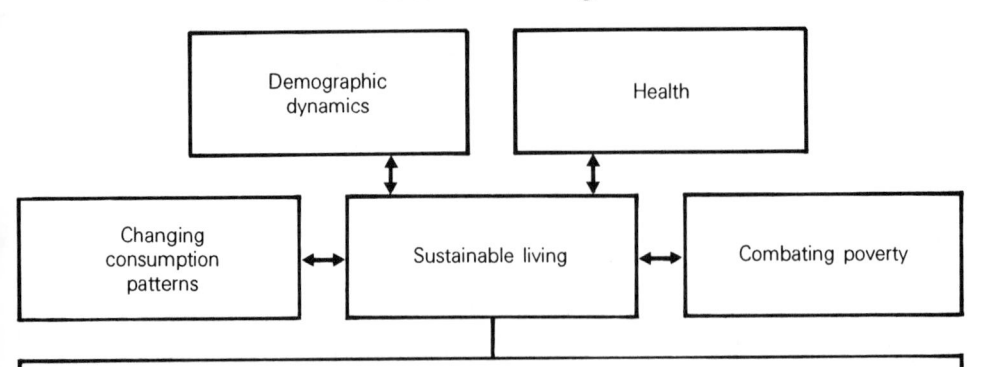

Sustainable living

```
┌─────────────────┐           ┌─────────────────┐
│   Demographic   │           │     Health      │
│    dynamics     │           │                 │
└────────┬────────┘           └────────┬────────┘
         │                             │
         ↕                             ↕
┌─────────────────┐  ┌─────────────────┐  ┌─────────────────┐
│   Changing      │  │                 │  │                 │
│   consumption   │←→│ Sustainable living │←→│ Combating poverty │
│    patterns     │  │                 │  │                 │
└─────────────────┘  └─────────────────┘  └─────────────────┘
```

Cross-sectoral linkages

Accelerating sustainable development: International trade; adequate net financial flows; domestic policies (ch. 1.1)

Integration of environment and development in decision-making: Policy, planning and management level; economic instruments and marketing incentives; environmental accounting; legal and regulatory frameworks (ch. 1.2)

Human settlements: Shelter; land and settlement management; environmental infrastructure; energy and transport; human resources and capacity-building; disaster-prone areas (ch. 3.1)

Urban water supplies: Drinking water; sanitation; intersectoral planning; monitoring (ch. 3.2)

Solid waste management: Waste minimization; safe disposal; expansion of services; recycling (ch. 3.3)

Urban pollution and health: Air pollution; municipal health planning; radiation protection (ch. 3.4)

Freshwater resources: Integrated assessment, development and management; protection of quality and resources; drinking water; sanitation (ch. 4.2)

Sustainable agriculture and rural development: Food security (ch. 4.3)

Managing fragile ecosystems: Combating desertification and drought Alternative livelihoods (ch. 4.5.1)
Sustainable mountain development Alternative livelihoods (ch. 4.5.2)

Environmentally sound management of biotechnology: Productivity of food and feed; health; environment protection (ch. 4.7)

Atmosphere: Sustainable energy development and consumption; transport systems; industry; agriculture; ozone depletion; addressing uncertainties (ch. 5.1)

Oceans and seas: Coastal area development (ch. 5.2)

Toxic chemicals: Chemical risks assessment; classification and labelling; information; risks management programmes (ch. 6.1)

Hazardous wastes: Cleaner production, waste minimization, institutional capacities; international cooperation for transboundary movement (ch. 6.2)

Radioactive wastes: International agreements for safe management (ch. 6.3)

Education, public awareness and training (ch. 7.1)

Strengthening the role of major groups: Women; youth; indigenous people and their communities; NGOs; farmers; local authorities; trade unions; business and industry; scientific and technological community (ch. 7.2)

in many cases, of their very cultural identity. Even in industrialized societies there are as many as 100 million poor people, many of whom are homeless and unemployed but have, at the very least, some access to social security benefits and health care.

Poverty in rural areas compels people to cultivate marginal lands, which results in soil erosion, depletion of shallow water resources and, consequently, lower crop yields, and tightens further the noose of poverty. Trying to survive on a daily basis, the poor have often little choice but to continue to overexploit their resources, which in turn reduces the chances of their offspring ever breaking free of the cycle of poverty and an unsustainable environment. Of the estimated 1 billion poor people living in developing regions, some 450 million live in low-potential agricultural areas. A similar number live in areas that are ecologically vulnerable, especially to soil erosion, land degradation, floods and other disasters; about 100 million others dwell in urban slums.

The poor are often the victims of environmental stresses caused by the actions of the rich. They are forced to live in areas more vulnerable to natural disasters, industrial hazards and water and air pollution. The growing migration from rural poverty to urban squalor is also of increasing concern, as this concentration of poverty leads to the breakdown of urban services and social systems, resulting in increased crime and a destabilizing socio-political environment. The burden of poverty and deprivation also falls far more heavily on women and children and certain ethnic and minority groups. These target groups require specific measures in poverty alleviation programmes.

An environmental policy that focuses mainly on the conservation and protection of resources, without due regard to the livelihoods of those who depend on them, would not only have an adverse impact on poverty but would also be unsuccessful. On the other hand, development policies that focus mainly on increasing production without concerning themselves with the long-term potential of the resources on which production is based would, sooner or later, run into problems of declining productivity and consequently greater poverty. An effective and sustainable development strategy to tackle the problems of poverty and environmental degradation should focus simultaneously on resources, production and people.

Governments, at the national and international level, need to provide the means and the commitment to combat poverty in all countries. A multifaceted strategy targeting the causes of poverty and focusing on vulnerable groups and fragile, low-potential ecosystems would require considerable funding and manpower resources. It should feature imaginative programmes to generate employment opportunities, as well as remunerative activities, and provide essential social services such as health, nutrition, education and safe water. The participation of local communities in the planning, formulation and implementation of such programmes is essential. Promoting the empowerment and improvement of the socioeconomic situation of vulnerable target groups, such as women, children, indigenous and minority communities, landless households, refugees and migrants, would also require specific priority measures.

Enabling the poor to achieve sustainable livelihoods should provide an integrating factor that allows policies to address issues of development, sustainable resource management and poverty eradication simultaneously. This would entail improving the means for information-gathering on poverty target groups and areas in order to facilitate the design of focused programmes. The programmes should work to equitably increase resource productivity; develop infrastructure, marketing systems, technologies and credit systems; and implement mechanisms for public participation to support and widen sustainable development options for resource-poor households.

Combating poverty involves promoting sustainable livelihoods. Programmes should cover a wide range of sectoral interventions and should be geographically and ecologically specific, aimed at specific vulnerable target groups and take into consideration the physical characteristics of the ecosystem concerned. They should include immediate steps to alleviate extreme poverty as well as long-term strategies for sustainable national socio-economic development to eliminate mass poverty and reduce inequalities.

A focal point in the United Nations system should be established to facilitate the exchange of information and the formulation and implementation of replicable pilot projects. In degraded and ecologically vulnerable areas, intensive efforts should be made to implement integrated policies and programmes for rehabilitating resource management and redressing poverty. This should involve development activities of lasting value, such as food-for-work programmes to build infrastructure. A review of the progress made in eradicating poverty through the implementation of the above activities should be given high priority in the follow-up of Agenda 21.

2.2 CHANGING CONSUMPTION PATTERNS

Economic growth is essential to meet basic human needs and achieve acceptable levels of personal well-being. Today's modern industrial economy has, however, led to the unprecedented use of energy and raw materials and the generation of wastes. Industrialized countries consume most of the world's energy, and many other resources, and far outstrip the consumption in developing countries.

Present levels of certain kinds of consumption, such as energy resources, in industrialized countries are already giving rise to serious environmental problems and are unlikely to be sustainable over the longer term. In addition, growing economies, incomes and population in the developing world seem destined to push human activities well beyond sustainable levels if similar consumption patterns take hold there. At the same time, consumption remains important as a driving force for development and for the creation of income and export markets needed to promote world-wide growth and prosperity.

This calls for a practical strategy to bring about a fundamental transition from the wasteful consumption patterns of the past to new consumption patterns based on efficiency and a concern for the future. In this respect, a new awareness and understanding, as well as a partnership between nations—industrial and developing—are crucial.

Since the mid-20th century, world energy production has risen some twentyfold; industrial output for the corresponding period has gone up some fourfold. Further, world population has doubled since then from 2.5 billion to 5.4 billion. This rapid growth in production has, for some, resulted in increased consumption and higher living standards. Most of this growth, however, has occurred in the developed countries, which, although comprising only one fifth of the total world population, account for some four fifths of the consumption of fossil fuels and other resources. Even with regard to the world's basic food commodities, such as cereals, meat and milk, industrialized countries consume between 48 and 72 per cent. Continuing these consumption levels in industrialized countries, while adopting them in developing countries, would not only be unsustainable but also gravely threaten the Earth's ecology. The world community needs to assess and curtail all wasteful and inefficient consumption patterns, particularly those that would seriously and irreparably damage our common environment.

Altering consumption patterns is one of the greatest challenges in the quest for environmentally sound and sustainable development, given the depth to which they are rooted in the basic values and lifestyles of industrial societies and emulated throughout much of the rest of the world. It requires the combined efforts of Governments, individuals and industry in a gradual process to examine new concepts of growth and prosperity which rely less on the flow of energy and natural resource materials through the economy and which take into account the availability and true value of natural resource capital.

The Governments and industries of many industrialized countries are intensifying their efforts to reduce the amount of resources used in the generation of economic growth, recognizing that this can both reduce environmental stress and contribute to greater economic and industrial competitiveness. Some progress has been achieved in making energy and raw material use more efficient through the adoption of environmentally sound technologies and recycling. These advances should be continued and generalized, and the experiences passed on to developing countries by helping them acquire these technologies, and develop others suited to their particular circumstances.

While the need to examine the role of consumption in dealing with environment and development is widely recognized, it is not yet matched by an understanding of the nature of the issue or how to address it. Governments and regional and international economic and environmental organizations, as well as private research and policy institutes, should make concerted efforts to compile basic data on consumption patterns and analyze the relationship between production, consumption, technological adaptation and innovation, economic growth and development, and population dynamics. Further, they should assess how modern economies can grow and prosper while reducing energy, material use and production of harmful wastes.

The costs and consequences of wasteful and environmentally damaging consumption are generally not borne fully by the producers and consumers who cause them. It is essential to design and implement market signals and sound environmental pricing that explicitly take into account the costs and consequences of consumption and waste generation. These may comprise environmental charges and taxes, deposit refund systems, emissions standards and charges and "polluter pays" principles. Governments should consider the adoption of such measures on a widespread and effective scale.

Information on the real environmental costs and consequences of various production processes and services can be critical in influencing and enabling consumers to make environmentally conscious product choices. These changes in demand will, in turn, also induce industry to adapt. Information dissemination and transparency are critical. Governments should review and improve the environmental impact of their procurement policies and encourage industry to introduce the environmental labelling of products, including energy, so that consumers can be clearly informed of the consequences of their consumption and behaviour.

The replication throughout the developing world of the present consumption patterns of industrialized countries is simply not a viable option, since this would place a tremendous stress on the Earth's environment. At the same time, levels of consumption in developing countries must increase in order to improve living standards. This has to be achieved through improving efficiencies, reducing wasteful consumption and the related waste generation. Without responsible attitudes and rational measures, both the consumption needs and living environment for future generations will be compromised.

2.3 DEMOGRAPHIC DYNAMICS AND SUSTAINABILITY

The world's population, in mid-1991, reached 5.4 billion, of which 77 per cent lived in developing countries and the rest in industrially advanced countries. In the 1960s, global population grew at about 2.1 per cent annually. This has now declined to some 1.7 per cent a year. The number of people added to the total each year, now amounting to 92 million, is higher than ever before. It is projected that world population will reach some 6.3 billion people in the year 2000 and 8.5 billion in the year 2025.

Over 90 per cent of the population increase today occurs in developing countries, having risen from 1.7 billion in 1950 to 4.2 billion in 1991, and expected to soar to nearly 5 billion by the year 2000.

By the turn of this century, some 2 billion people in the developing world will live in urban areas: over 40 per cent of the people in Africa and Asia—excluding Japan—and 76 per cent of those in Latin America will be urbanized. Of the world's 20 largest cities, 17 will be in the developing countries. At present, over 40 per cent of the urban population in the developing world lives in squalor, without access to essential services such as health care. Coping with these projected urban populations in the future poses major challenges to sustainable development.

Rapidly increasing demands for natural resources, employment, education and social services will make it difficult to protect natural resources and improve living standards. The migration of large numbers of people within countries and across national boundaries will, more than likely, continue to increase, driven by a combination of factors, including population growth, concentration of wealth and land, poverty and economic polarization.

Developmental and environmental conservation plans have generally recognized population variables as critical factors which influence consumption patterns, production, lifestyles and long-term sustainability. But more attention will have to be given to these issues in general policy formulation and the design of development plans. All countries will have to improve their capacities to assess the environmental and developmental implications of their population patterns, and to formulate and implement appropriate policies and action programmes. These policies should be designed to cope with the inevitable increase in population numbers, while at the same time incorporating measures to bring about the demographic transition.

Population programmes are at the interface between people and their environment. Local-level sustainability requires a new action framework that examines population dynamics in conjunction with other factors such as the social dimensions of gender, access to resources, livelihoods and the structure of authority. Population programmes should empower people, and be consistent with socio-economic and environmental planning for sustainability. Integrated population/environment programmes should closely correlate action on demographic variables with resources management activities and development goals.

A major priority is *developing and disseminating knowledge concerning the links between demographic trends and factors and sustainable development.* Population dynamics must be incorporated in the global analysis and research of environment and development issues. Governments should work to develop a better understanding of the relationships between human populations, technology, cultural behaviour, natural capital and life-support systems. In order to determine the priorities for action at global and regional levels, human vulnerability in sensitive areas and centres of population must be carefully assessed.

Another priority is *formulating integrated national policies for environment and development, taking into account demographic trends and factors.* National population issues must be integrated into the national planning, policy and decision-making process as part of national development and conservation plans. Policies and programmes should combine environment and development issues with population concerns to foster a holistic view of sustainable development that holds as its goals the alleviation of poverty, secure livelihoods, integrated health care, the reduction of maternal and infant mortality, education and services for the responsible planning of family size, the improvement of the status and income of women, the fulfilment of women's personal aspirations and individual and community empowerment. These policies and programmes should be people-centred, working to increase the quality and improve the capacity of human resources for environmental conservation.

Lastly, *implementing integrated environment and development programmes at the local level, taking into account demographic trends and factors* is also a critical priority. These programmes should work to improve the quality of life, ensure the sustainable use of natural resources and enhance environmental quality.

These priorities will require the strengthening of research activities that integrate population and environment issues, such as integrated demographic analysis, which embraces a broad social science perspective of environmental changes, and models methodologies and socio-demographic information in a suitable format for interfacing with physical and biological data. They will also require increased awareness of the need to sustain the world's resources through the rationalization of resource use, consumption patterns and population. Better "population literacy"—an awareness of the population/environment interactions taking place at local and national levels—should be developed among decision-makers, parliamentarians, journalists, teachers and students, civil and religious authorities and the general public.

To strengthen institutional capacity, Governments should promote the collaborative exchange of information between research institutions and international, regional and national agencies involved in population programmes. Governments should enhance national capacities to deal with integrated population/environment/development issues by strengthening population committees and commissions, population planning units, and advisory committees on population to enable them to elaborate population policies consistent with national strategies for sustainable development.

2.4 PROTECTING AND PROMOTING HUMAN HEALTH CONDITIONS

Poor health and disease are endemic in the developing—and mainly tropical—countries. This is, to a large extent, the result of poverty, a lack of basic health services, crowded and poorly serviced housing, illiteracy and ignorance and rapidly multiplying populations. Poverty remains the most significant predictor of urban and rural morbidity and mortality. The strong association between poverty and ill-health is evident in the widespread incidence of communicable and non-communicable diseases among the poor, especially in the developing countries.

Underdevelopment is often linked to the poor maintenance of general hygiene and sanitation and inadequate management of the environment. This accounts for the prevalence in the developing world of such parasitic diseases as malaria and schistosomiasis, onchocerciasis (river blindness) and other vector-borne diseases. Due to inaction, African trypanosomiasis (sleeping sickness) continues to take a heavy toll. Efforts to reduce communicable diseases in these countries may have no effect, or even backfire, if development efforts aggravate environmental problems such as deforestation, the alteration of hydrological systems, soil erosion, desertification and the changes in population movements and habitats that ensue. The epidemiology of these diseases is determined by the social, cultural and economic activities of the people and the ecosystems they inhabit. The public health importance of each disease varies from one developing country to another, and lack of development will have different impacts on their progression, extension and aggravation.

Health depends ultimately on the ability to successfully manage the interactions between the physical, biological, economic and social environments. The condition of the health sector both helps determine, and is dependent on, the overall development of social and economic conditions. It is also dependent on a healthy environment, including the provision of clean water, sanitation, adequate food supplies and proper nutrition. These criteria require the building of a primary health care infrastructure in conjunction with primary environmental care.

Although sound development is impossible without a healthy population, most development, to some degree, harms the environment and indirectly causes or exacerbates health problems. Underdevelopment is both the cause and effect of inadequate health in developing countries. Meeting basic health needs, therefore, goes hand in hand with the alleviation of poverty, and should be seen as a contribution to it. The fundamental objective for Governments should be to achieve "Health for All" by the year 2000 to meet the basic health needs of all the world's people. As a matter of priority, health service coverage should be achieved for population groups that are in greatest need.

Meeting primary health care needs, particularly in rural areas, involves setting up primary health care technologies which are practicable, scientifically sound and geared to the needs of individual countries. Coordination among the sectors for public health, environmental protection and development planning should be strengthened at local and national levels. Health facilities, aided by mechanisms for sustained local community involvement, should be established and monitored, especially at the district level, and their medical and social services staff trained to deliver basic health care. Traditional knowledge of preventive and curative health practices can often support health care initiatives for the self-management of local communities.

National coordinated action plans and monitoring mechanisms should be established for the *control of communicable diseases* such as malaria, diarrhoeal diseases, hepatitis, sleeping sickness, soil-transmitted helminths, schistosomiasis and acute respiratory diseases. Specific targets to be achieved by the year 2000 include the eradication of polio and guineaworm disease, or dracunculiasis, and the effective control of onchocerciasis and leprosy. A global monitoring system for endemic diseases, particularly those with a potential for transboundary spread, should be established by the year 2000.

National and regional institutions should promote broad intersectoral approaches to prevent and control communicable diseases, including applying new vaccines and chemotherapeutic agents, developing information for public awareness and education, and providing training in immunology, molecular biology, epidemiology and community prevention and control. National and international efforts against the Acquired Immune Deficiency Syndrome (AIDS) are essential to prevent and reduce the social impacts of infection by the Human Immunodeficiency Virus (HIV).

Specific health measures for *protecting vulnerable groups*, particularly infants, youth, women and indigenous people and their communities, include: strengthening immunization and nutrition programmes; treating and preventing communicable diseases; providing social services for the education, counselling and treatment of specific health problems, including drug abuse; incorporating health issues in national action programmes on women and development; and utilizing women's groups at the community and national levels in all aspects of health care.

The development of human resources to protect the health of children, youth, women and indigenous people and their communities should include strengthening educational institutions, promoting interactive methods of education for health, and increasing the use of mass media in disseminating information to target groups. This requires the training of more community health workers, nurses, midwives, physicians, social scientists and educators; the education of mothers, families and communities; and the strengthening of ministries of education, health and population.

New approaches to planning and managing health care systems and facilities should be field-tested, and research on ways of integrating appropriate technologies into health infrastructures supported. Sound health technology should be developed that is both adaptable to local needs as well as maintainable and, in the case of equipment, repairable by local community resources.

Governments should intensify and expand their multidisciplinary health research, including focused efforts on the mitigation and environmental control of the vectors of tropical diseases and intervention studies on how to provide a solid epidemiological basis for control policies and evaluate the efficiency of alternatives. This should also include investigating possible epidemiological, social and economic bases for the development of more effective national strategies for the integrated environmental control of communicable diseases. Social research on the unique problems of vulnerable groups should be expanded and methods for implementing flexible, pragmatic solutions should be explored, with an emphasis on preventive measures. Technical support should also be provided to Governments, institutions, youth and women's nongovernmental organizations in the health sector.

Intersectoral approaches to the reform of health personnel development, including managerial skills at the local community level, should be strengthened to ensure they will contribute to meeting the "Health for All" objective and to ensure the systematic development and efficient operation of the health system. Finally, Governments need to adopt enabling and facilitating strategies, both to provide communities with health care services and to help them meet their own needs.

3

HUMAN SETTLEMENTS

SHORTLY after the turn of this century, nearly one half of the global population will live in cities. This urbanization of society into human settlements is an expected outcome of development. It opens new opportunities for society, enabling the efficient provision of basic services. Generating some 60 per cent of the global gross national product, cities are a major force behind national economic growth. In developing countries, cities are growing by some 60 million inhabitants annually, a pattern that will lead to a net doubling of urban populations in the next 25 years. This has put enormous pressure on urban infrastructures already under serious stress and unable to meet the needs of the existing inhabitants. Overcrowding, insufficient housing, lack of access to clean water and sanitation, growing amounts of uncollected waste and deteriorating air quality are already serious problems in these cities and may worsen substantially if effective and timely action is not taken.

The concentration of people in urban areas presents complex planning and management problems in environmental health, energy and transportation, water supplies and waste management. There is a need to develop policies that can connect public, private and social sectors and the institutions to provide training of technical experts and planners.

Environmental health considerations should be incorporated into all aspects of urban development policy. Factors include noise pollution, radiation and waste from factories and power plants. Technology and infrastructure are needed to monitor air and water quality, and stringent anti-pollution laws need to be enacted and enforced.

Indoor smoke from wood fires and coal stoves is a major health hazard for millions of urban dwellers in developing countries. Economic incentives and education campaigns are important to get people to switch to healthier methods of cooking and heating their homes.

Rapid urban population growth is also endangering the quality and supply of water. It is important that all urban residents have access to safe water. The treatment and safe disposal of an increasing proportion of solid wastes, including sewage, needs priority attention. In the industrialized countries, this involves avoiding the discharge of sludge into rivers and seas. In developing countries, less than 10 per cent of urban waste receives any treatment, and only a small fraction of this meets any acceptable quality standards. Countries need to establish waste disposal standards, based on the local capacity of the environment to assimilate the waste produced. New approaches should be developed to collect, store and dispose of urban wastes.

A phased and coordinated approach is essential, from the governmental to the individual level, to ensure the provision of essential infrastructure and services, such as housing, transport, clean water, municipal waste management, health services and employment and income-remunerative activities. Policy planning and management in these areas should include not only the present inhabitants but also those expected to arrive in the coming decades. It is only through such a comprehensive approach that Governments can effectively address the complex problems of sustainable urban development and tap the full economic and social potential that their cities offer.

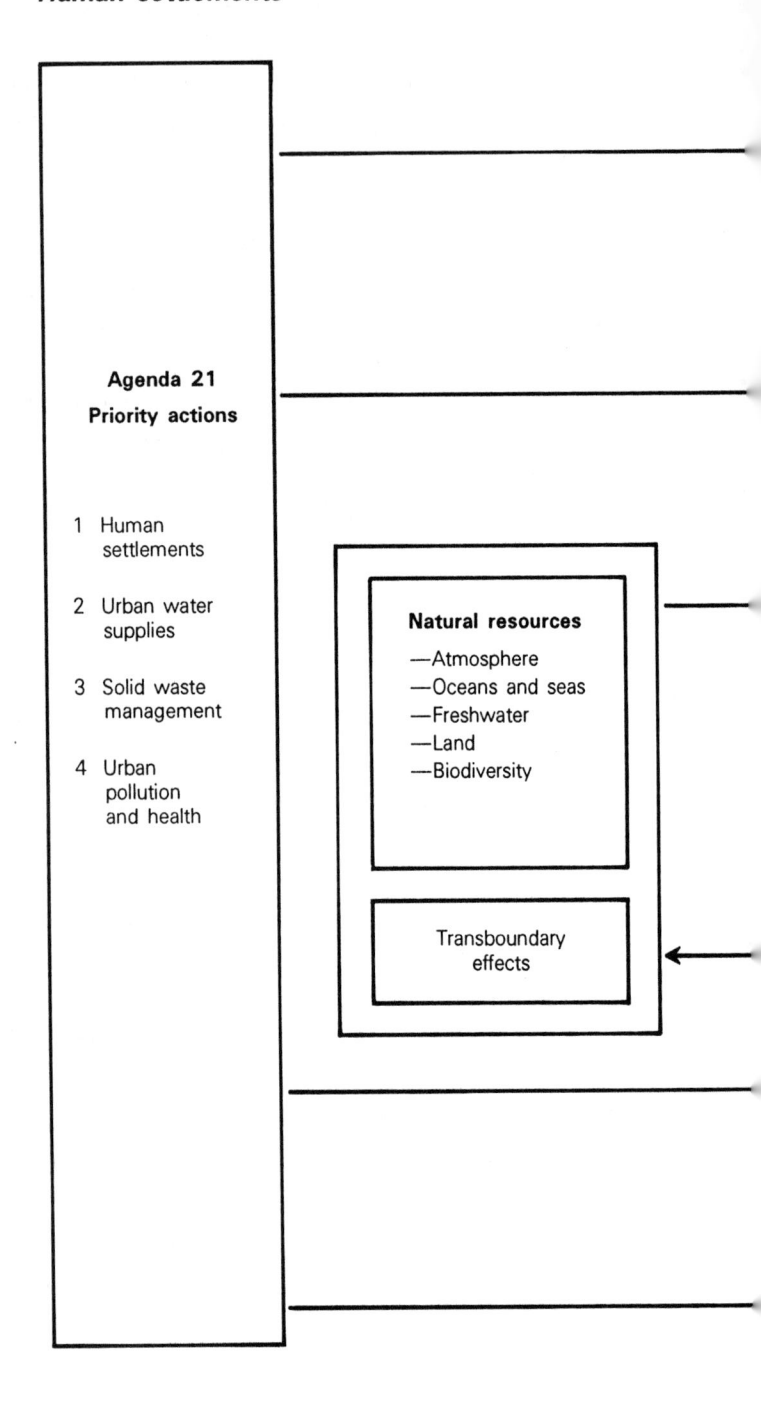

Human settlements

Agenda 21
Priority actions

1 Human settlements

2 Urban water supplies

3 Solid waste management

4 Urban pollution and health

Natural resources
—Atmosphere
—Oceans and seas
—Freshwater
—Land
—Biodiversity

Transboundary effects

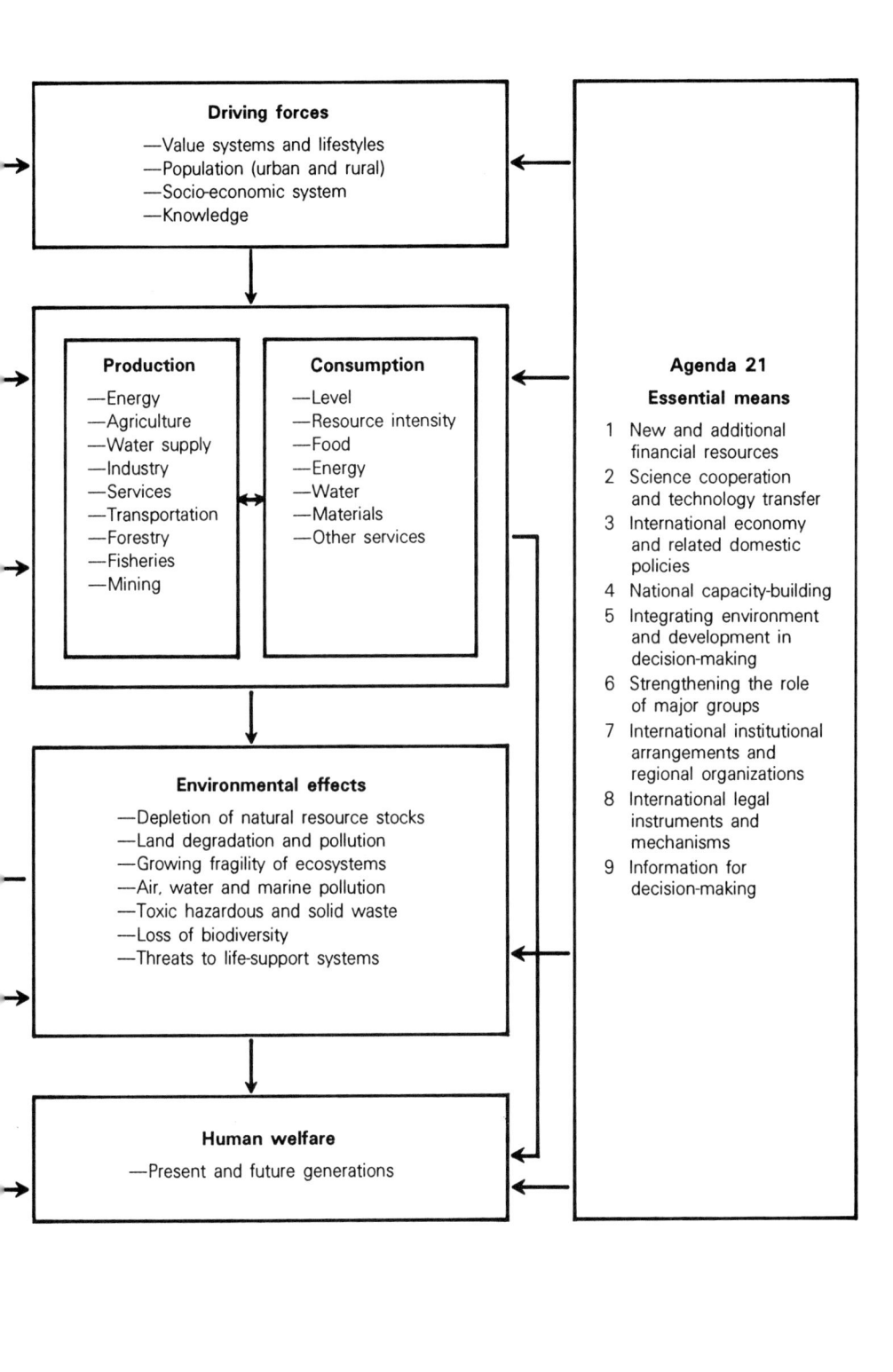

Driving forces
- Value systems and lifestyles
- Population (urban and rural)
- Socio-economic system
- Knowledge

Production
- Energy
- Agriculture
- Water supply
- Industry
- Services
- Transportation
- Forestry
- Fisheries
- Mining

Consumption
- Level
- Resource intensity
- Food
- Energy
- Water
- Materials
- Other services

Environmental effects
- Depletion of natural resource stocks
- Land degradation and pollution
- Growing fragility of ecosystems
- Air, water and marine pollution
- Toxic hazardous and solid waste
- Loss of biodiversity
- Threats to life-support systems

Human welfare
- Present and future generations

Agenda 21
Essential means
1. New and additional financial resources
2. Science cooperation and technology transfer
3. International economy and related domestic policies
4. National capacity-building
5. Integrating environment and development in decision-making
6. Strengthening the role of major groups
7. International institutional arrangements and regional organizations
8. International legal instruments and mechanisms
9. Information for decision-making

Human settlements

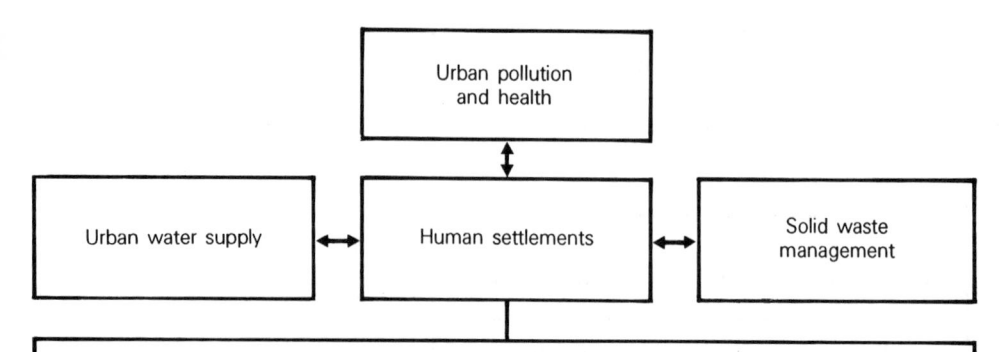

```
              ┌──────────────────┐
              │  Urban pollution │
              │    and health    │
              └────────┬─────────┘
                       ↕
┌──────────────┐  ┌────────────────┐  ┌──────────────┐
│ Urban water  │↔ │ Human          │ ↔│ Solid waste  │
│   supply     │  │ settlements    │  │ management   │
└──────────────┘  └────────┬───────┘  └──────────────┘
                           │
```

Cross-sectoral linkages

Accelerating sustainable development: International trade; adequate net financial flows; domestic policies (ch. 1.1)

Integration of environment and development in decision-making: Policy, planning and management level; economic instruments and marketing incentives; environmental accounting; legal and regulatory frameworks (ch. 1.2)

Combating poverty: Providing sustainable livelihoods (ch. 2.1)

Changing consumption patterns: Less wasteful lifestyles; sustainable consumption levels; informed consumer choices (ch. 2.2)

Demographic dynamic pressures: National and local level integration of population and environment (ch. 2.3)

Health: Pollution health risks; basic needs; communicable diseases; vulnerable groups (ch. 2.4)

Land resources: Integrated planning and management (ch. 4.1)

Freshwater resources: Integrated assessment, development and management; protection of quality and resources; drinking water; sanitation (ch. 4.2)

Sustainable agriculture and rural development: Rural employment; food security (ch. 4.3)

Atmosphere: Sustainable energy development and consumption; transport systems; industry; agriculture; ozone depletion; addressing uncertainties (ch. 5.1)

Oceans and seas: Coastal area development (ch. 5.2)

Toxic chemicals: Chemical risks assessment; classification and labelling; information; risks management programmes (ch. 6.1)

Hazardous wastes: Cleaner production, waste minimization, institutional capacities; international cooperation for transboundary movement (ch. 6.2)

Radioactive wastes: International agreements for safe management (ch. 6.3)

Education, public awareness and training: (ch. 7.1)

Strengthening the role of major groups: Women; youth; indigenous people and their communities; NGOs; farmers; local authorities; trade unions; business and industry; scientific and technological community (ch. 7.2)

3.1 PROMOTING SUSTAINABLE HUMAN SETTLEMENT DEVELOPMENT

Urban human settlements absorb two thirds of the total population increase in the developing world. At this rate, close to 2 billion people will populate the urban areas of developing countries by the year 2000, of which some 600 million will have been added during the 1990s alone. Another 2 billion are expected to be added to the urban population of developing countries in the quarter century from 2000 to 2025.

Cities are major catalysts of economic growth in developing countries. Economic activities tend to concentrate in the urban centres where today one third of the total population generates some 60 per cent of the gross national product. Better urban management can ameliorate living conditions, improve natural resources, sustainably support rural development and accelerate national growth. Cities can provide health, education and social services not only to their own residents but also to many more people who cannot find adequate services in smaller settlements and sparsely populated rural areas.

As the physical environment in and around growing cities deteriorates, those affected most are the urban poor the "marginalized and disenfranchised" who make up over a third of the urban population in developing countries and whose numbers are rapidly growing. For most city dwellers in the developing countries, living conditions are worsening as a result of the inability of the city or national Government to provide satisfactory services for drinking water, sanitation, solid waste disposal, transport and energy for cooking and heating. For the urban poor, the priorities are improved housing, provision of basic health care and water and sanitation services at affordable costs.

Shelter is fundamental to an individual's physical, psychological, social and economic well-being. The Global Strategy for Shelter to the Year 2000, adopted by the United Nations General Assembly in December 1988, requires much greater political and financial support and technical assistance to enable it to reach its goal of *providing adequate shelter for all* by the end of this century. Developing countries should adopt national shelter strategies focused on the use of new and innovative financing mechanisms, such as specific housing schemes. They should support the shelter efforts of poor and vulnerable groups by facilitating their access to land, reforming existing codes and regulations, financing and building materials and actively promoting the regularization and upgrading of informal settlements. At the national level, the implementation of these national shelter strategies should be monitored and adapted to changing conditions.

Improving human settlement management in developing countries should be through the implementation of integrated urban development programmes. These programmes should adopt measures to generate employment opportunities for the poor, through the provision, improvement and maintenance of urban infrastructure and services and the support of informal sector activities such as repairs, recycling, services and small commerce. The social infrastructure should be developed to reduce hunger and homelessness and provide adequate health care, education and other services. Local, national and international urban data collection, dissemination and management capabilities should be built up to facilitate reviews of urbanization processes and policies and identify local urban growth factors. To improve local planning and management, authorities must adopt a participatory approach to sustainable urban development, that promotes continuous dialogue between the public sector, the private sector and local communities.

In providing land for human settlements and *promoting sustainable land-use planning and management* policies, developing countries need to compile a comprehensive national inventory of their land resources and develop urban land resource management plans which implement integrated land-use policies that take into account the conflicting demands of industry, housing, commerce, agriculture and the need for open spaces, as well as the rising costs of urban land. Coordination is essential to ensure the poor are not denied access to suitable land: when expanding urban slums encroach on peripheral, unsuitable land, they threaten the social and economic fabric of urban life. At the international level, the sharing of relevant experiences on sustainable urban land management practices, especially among developing countries, should be facilitated.

Urban land-use planning and *promoting the integrated provision of environmental infrastructure—water, sanitation, drainage and solid-waste management*—in all human settlements is essential for environmental protection, increased productivity, better health and poverty alleviation. Developing countries should ensure that all municipal departments coordinate their efforts, such as capacity-building, monitoring, applied research, and using appropriate technology and technical expertise. In addition, developing countries should adopt an integrated approach to the provision of water supply, sanitation, drainage and solid waste management in all urban areas, including informal settlements, where standards and regulations are best adapted to the living conditions and resources of the urban poor.

At a global level, most energy is derived from fossils fuels and is used in urban areas. Transport accounts for close to 30 per cent of global commercial energy consumption and about 60 per cent of the total global consumption of liquid petroleum. In developing countries, rapid motorization and the lack of resources for investment in urban transport planning, traffic management and infrastructure have combined to create increasing health, noise, congestion and productivity problems.

Developing countries are at present faced with the need to increase their energy production to accelerate development and raise the living standards of their populations, while reducing energy production costs and energy-related pollution. Increasing the efficiency of energy use to reduce its polluting effects and to promote the use of renewable energies must be a priority in any action taken to promote the urban environment. The objective in *promoting sustainable energy and transport systems in human settlements* is to extend the provision of more energy-efficient technology and alternative/renewable energy for human settlements and to reduce negative impacts of energy production and use on human health and on the environment.

The construction industry, which provides shelter, infrastructure and employment, is vital to the achievement of national socio-economic development goals. But it can also damage the environment by degrading fragile eco-zones, using harmful materials, consuming excessive energy and increasing air pollution. In *promoting sustainable construction industry activities*, developing countries should encourage the use of local materials and labour-intensive construction methods to generate employment. They should adopt measures to make building materials more affordable to the urban and rural poor, through credit schemes and bulk procurement of building materials, such as recycled construction materials, for sale to small-scale builders and communities. Developed countries should create and disseminate databases on the adverse environmental effects of building materials and introduce regulatory measures on the use of non-renewable natural resources, such as tropical hardwoods, in construction. Technologies and experiences should be exchanged and shared among developing and industrialized countries.

In many parts of the world, the toll of natural and manmade disasters has been unacceptably high. *Promoting human settlement planning and management in disaster-prone areas* involves a range of measures, including media campaigns to build public awareness, early warning systems, guidelines on the location, design and operation of potentially hazardous industries, and better building and construction technologies. In highly disaster-prone areas, emergency preparedness and strategies for post-disaster reconstruction and resettlement, incorporating past experience, are essential.

In all of these priority activities, the overriding need to ameliorate the living conditions of the expanding low-income and poor urban communities in developing countries involves *promoting human resource development and capacity-building for human settlement development.* It is important to create an enabling policy environment supportive of the partnership between the public, private and community sectors and to reorient the national training curricula of technicians, professionals and administrators whose work relates to human settlements development at the community level.

3.2 URBAN WATER SUPPLIES

Early in the next century, more than half of the world's population will be living in urban areas. By the year 2025, that proportion will have risen to 60 per cent, comprising some 5 billion people. Rapid urban population growth and industrialization are putting severe strains on water resources for human consumption and industrial use. Special attention needs to be given to the growing effects of urbanization on water demands and usage and to the critical role played by local and municipal authorities in managing the supply, use and overall treatment of water, particularly in developing countries for which special support is needed. A high proportion of large urban agglomerations are located around estuaries and coastal zones, leading to municipal and industrial pollution and over-exploitation of available water resources, which together threaten both the marine environment and supply of freshwater resources. Better management of urban water resources, including the elimination of unsustainable consumption patterns, is essential for the alleviation of poverty and the improvement of the health and quality of life of the urban population. In developing countries, specific measures such as low-cost water supply, sanitation, and waste management programmes need to be directed toward the large numbers of the urban poor.

The overall strategy for *water and sustainable urban development* should identify and implement strategies and actions to ensure the continued supply of affordable water for present and future needs, and to reverse current trends of resource degradation and depletion. In particular, activities should aim to ensure that, by the year 2000, all urban residents have access to at least 40 litres per head per day of safe water, that 75 per cent of the urban population are provided with on-site or community facilities for sanitation, and that the solid waste generated in urban areas is collected and recycled or disposed of in an environmentally safe way. The specific actions needed to satisfy this priority are indicated below.

Water resources should be protected through the introduction of sanitary waste disposal facilities based on ecologically sound, low-cost and upgradable technologies, urban storm water run-off and drainage programmes, the promotion of recycling and reuse of wastewater and solid wastes and the control of sources of industrial pollution. The rehabilitation of malfunctioning systems and the correction of operation and maintenance inadequacies should be considered. City development planning should be consistent with the sustainable management of water resources and satisfy the basic water needs of the urban population. This may involve the introduction of water tariffs, where affordable, to reflect the marginal and opportunity cost of water, especially in production. Throughout these programmes, the skills and potential of non-governmental organizations, the private sector and local people should be utilized, taking into account public and strategic interests in water resources. The public should also be made aware of the social and economic value of water, and encouraged to use it rationally and protect its quality. Governments should develop legislation and policies to promote investment in urban water supplies and solid waste and sewage management by encouraging the autonomy and financial viability of utilities and providing training for professional personnel.

A prerequisite for progress in enhancing access to water and sanitation services is the establishment of an institutional framework which ensures that the real needs of presently unserved populations are reflected in urban development planning. The multi-sectoral approach, which is a vital part of urban water resources management, requires institutional linkages at national and city levels, including inter-sectoral planning groups. Pollution control and prevention depend on the integration of economic and regulatory mechanisms, backed by adequate monitoring and surveillance.

3.3 ENVIRONMENTALLY SOUND MANAGEMENT OF SOLID WASTES AND SEWAGE-RELATED ISSUES

Municipal solid wastes include domestic refuse and non-hazardous wastes such as commercial and institutional wastes, street sweepings and construction debris. By the end of this century, over 1 billion people will be without sufficient solid waste disposal services. Inadequate services can lead not only to the serious, long-term pollution of land, air and water resources, but also to bacterial and parasitic infections, affecting the health of the urban poor with particular severity. At present, as many as 5 million people—of whom nearly 4 million are under the age of 5 years—die each year from waste-related diseases. The waste problem is especially severe in the rapidly growing informal settlements of the developing world, where population densities and health risks are high, public awareness of the hazards of uncontrolled disposal is low and the consequent need for municipal waste disposal services is greatest. These health and environmental effects, moreover, are felt far beyond the unserved settlements themselves in the form of water, land and air contamination and pollution over a wide area. Extending and improving waste collection, together with appropriate processing and safe disposal services, is, therefore, necessary and vital.

By the year 2025, with over 5.5 billion people expected to live in urban areas, waste generation is likely to increase some fivefold. This may be accompanied by a decrease in the bio-degradability of wastes, as larger amounts of non-organic materials and industrial wastes are discharged into municipal waste facilities. The best chance of reversing this trend is to address its root cause and alter unsustainable patterns of production and consumption through the application of the integrated life-cycle management concept. In this context, development and environment are taken into account throughout the life-cycle of any given product, from design and production to recycling and disposal. A strategy for waste prevention, minimization and reuse would become the basis for all future solid waste management programmes. Waste minimization can be achieved by modifying industrial processes and changes in the design and use of products.

While the inadequate disposal of wastes gives rise to several environmental problems that contribute to unsustainable patterns of development, sound waste management policies provide exceptional opportunities for enhancing the environment and supporting development. For example, recycling metal, paper, glass, plastics and organic wastes can lessen the demand for energy, raw materials and fertilizers.

The environmentally sound management of solid wastes requires the integration of four interrelated priority areas, along with the collaboration of national Governments and institutions, and inter-governmental and non-governmental organizations. The mix and emphasis given to each of these four areas varies according to the local socio-economic and physical conditions, rates of waste generation and their composition.

The first priority is *minimizing wastes*, particularly wastes destined for final disposal, by formulating waste reduction goals based on weight, volume and composition. With the co-operation of international organizations, Governments should strengthen their procedures for assessing waste quantity and composition changes as well as enacting waste minimization policies. This should include developing and strengthening national capacities and incentives to reduce unsustainable production and consumption patterns as well as developing and applying methodologies for national waste monitoring and processing.

The second priority is *maximizing environmentally sound waste reuse and recycling*. Government departments, non-governmental organizations, consumers, women and youth groups, in collaboration with appropriate international organizations, should launch programmes to demonstrate and implement enhanced waste reuse and recycling. These programmes should include small-scale cottage-based recycling industries, compost production, treated wastewater irrigation and energy recovery from waste. Information, techniques and appropriate policy instruments must be made available to encourage the adoption of these schemes.

In many developing countries, over 90 per cent of urban waste is left untreated prior to disposal. As a third priority, therefore, Governments, non-governmental organizations and industries, in collaboration with appropriate international organizations, should launch programmes for *promoting environmentally sound waste disposal and treatment*. The international community should also generate the necessary information, including disposal criteria, and provide the technology and financial support for encouraging the treatment and safe disposal of wastes in all countries.

Finally, the fourth priority of *extending waste service coverage* should provide health-protecting and environmentally safe waste collection and disposal services covering all urban and rural areas. This should involve the full range of low-cost options for waste management, fully integrated into codes of practice and regulation with other basic services, such as water supply.

Improving solid waste management requires changes in technical, social, financial, planning, legislative and institutional practices at the community, local, national, regional and global levels. Implementing such changes will require considerable efforts to build up sufficient capacity within relevant institutions and organizations. Education, training, institutional reform and information exchange are some of the means by which local and national Governments can strengthen their capacity to manage wastes. Capacity-building programmes need to involve a variety of individuals, including officials, professionals, technicians, researchers, educators, public and private sector institutions, non-governmental organizations, community organizations and the public at large.

3.4 URBAN POLLUTION AND HEALTH

Swift global urbanization has outstripped society's capacity to meet basic human needs, leaving hundreds of millions of people—particularly in developing countries—with inadequate incomes, diets, housing and services. The financial resources and administrative capacity of municipal authorities often cannot meet the increasing need for environmental health services. Environmental pollution in urban areas is associated with excess morbidity and mortality, while overcrowding and inadequate housing in the peri-urban areas contribute to respiratory diseases, tuberculosis, meningitis and other diseases.

In many locations around the world the general environment—air, water and land—is so badly polluted that the health of hundreds of millions of people is adversely affected. This is due to past and present developments in consumption and production patterns and lifestyles, in energy production and use, in industry and in transportation, with little or no regard for environmental protection. There have, however, been notable improvements in some countries, but deterioration of the environment continues.

Urban growth has short- and long-term environmental impacts, and consequent implications for health. In *meeting the urban health challenge*, it is important to minimize conflicts between economic development (necessary for improving human health) and environmental protection (on which depends the long-term maintenance of human health). Supportive environments for health have to be created in the urban settlements.

The priority in urban areas for *reducing health risks from environmental pollution and hazards* should be to maintain the environment to a degree that human health and safety are not impaired and yet encourage development to proceed. Specific programmes to incorporate appropriate environmental and health safeguards as part of national and urban development programmes include establishing adequate national infrastructures and programmes for providing requisite pollution surveillance, information gathering on health effects to support cost-benefit analyses and environmental health impact assessments to help determine pollution control, prevention and abatement measures.

Appropriate air pollution control technologies should be developed on the basis of risk assessment and epidemiological research considered as part of the introduction of clean production processes and suitable safe mass transport. Air pollution control capacities emphasizing monitoring networks and enforcement programmes should be installed in all major cities. Prevention and control methods are required to reduce indoor air pollution, including the provision of economic incentives for the installation of appropriate technology. This should be supported by health education campaigns in developing countries to reduce the health impact of domestic use of biomass and coal. Further, the effective prevention of adverse health effects from ionizing and non-ionizing radiation necessitates the development and implementation of national radiation protection legislation, standards and enforcement procedures on the basis of existing international guidelines.

In all national programmes for pollution control and management, Governments should establish environmental health impact assessment procedures for the planning and development of new industries and energy facilities, including health risk analysis. Industrial hygiene programmes are also needed in all major industries for the surveillance of workers' exposure to health hazards, noting especially the need to protect female workers. Strategies to reduce the frequency and severity of exposure have to be developed and implemented in industry, traffic and other accident-prone sectors. To further enhance workers' safety, preventive measures should be taken to reduce occupationally-derived diseases caused by environmental and occupational toxins.

Water pollution control efforts should aim at the integrated environmentally sound management of water resources and the safe disposal of liquid and solid wastes. This should include the establishment of protected areas for sources of water supply, the safe disposal of refuse, the control of water-associated diseases and the sanitary disposal of excreta and sewage, using appropriate systems to treat wastewater in urban and rural areas. Waterborne diseases and contamination of drinking water can, in this way, be reduced to safe levels.

To enhance municipal health planning, city authorities should establish intersectoral committees at both the political and technical level, as a way of forming collaborative networks with scientific, cultural, medical, business, social and other city institutions. These "Healthy City" networks should be expanded and maintained to ensure collaboration and the exchange of information and experience.

With regard to the promotion of research, priority should be given to developing new methods for the quantitative assessment of benefits and costs associated with different pollution control strategies, and expanding interdisciplinary research on the combined health effects of exposure to multiple environmental hazards. This should include epidemiological investigations on long-term exposure to low levels of pollutants and the use of biological markers capable of estimating human exposure, adverse effects, and susceptibility to environmental agents. The "polluter pays" principle should be applied rigorously, and economic incentives for pollution control developed.

Improvement in urban development and management requires better national and municipal statistics based on practical, standardized indicators. The aim should be to develop methods to measure intra-urban and intra-district variations in health status and environmental conditions, and to apply this information in planning and management. This will allow the targeting of environmental health measures at population groups whose need is greatest, and who are especially vulnerable to the effects of pollution.

All countries should develop the knowledge and practical skills to foresee and identify urban environmental health hazards, and the capacity to reduce the risks. Basic capacity requirements must include enhanced public awareness; knowledge about environmental health problems; operational mechanisms for intersectoral and intergovernmental cooperation in planning, management and combating pollution; and arrangements for involving private industry and community interests.

4

EFFICIENT RESOURCE USE

ENVIRONMENTAL changes normally occur over geological time under the influence of natural forces. Increasing human activities, however, have put an additional load on these natural forces, considerably stressing the environment and threatening the Earth's fertility. Growing demands on land resources have led to soil erosion, salinization and waterlogging, desertification, deforestation and the disruption of many precious and economically vital ecosystems. The pollution and overuse of the world's finite freshwater resources threaten all socio-economic sectors.

An integrated approach to land use should be employed at all stages of decision-making, from goal-setting to implementation. Legislation, regulations and economic incentives should encourage the rational use of land. Research is also important to determine the capacity of land and the interaction among various land uses and environmental processes.

Overdependence on non-renewable fossil fuels as a primary source of energy has contributed to air pollution, acid rain, greenhouse warming, marine pollution and other adverse impacts. The level of these pollutants in the environment poses a threat not just to human health but to forests, mountains, lakes and rivers, as well as their fragile ecosystems. It is unlikely that fossil fuels will be abandoned in the near future. Improvements, however, can be made in energy efficiency while

Efficient resource use

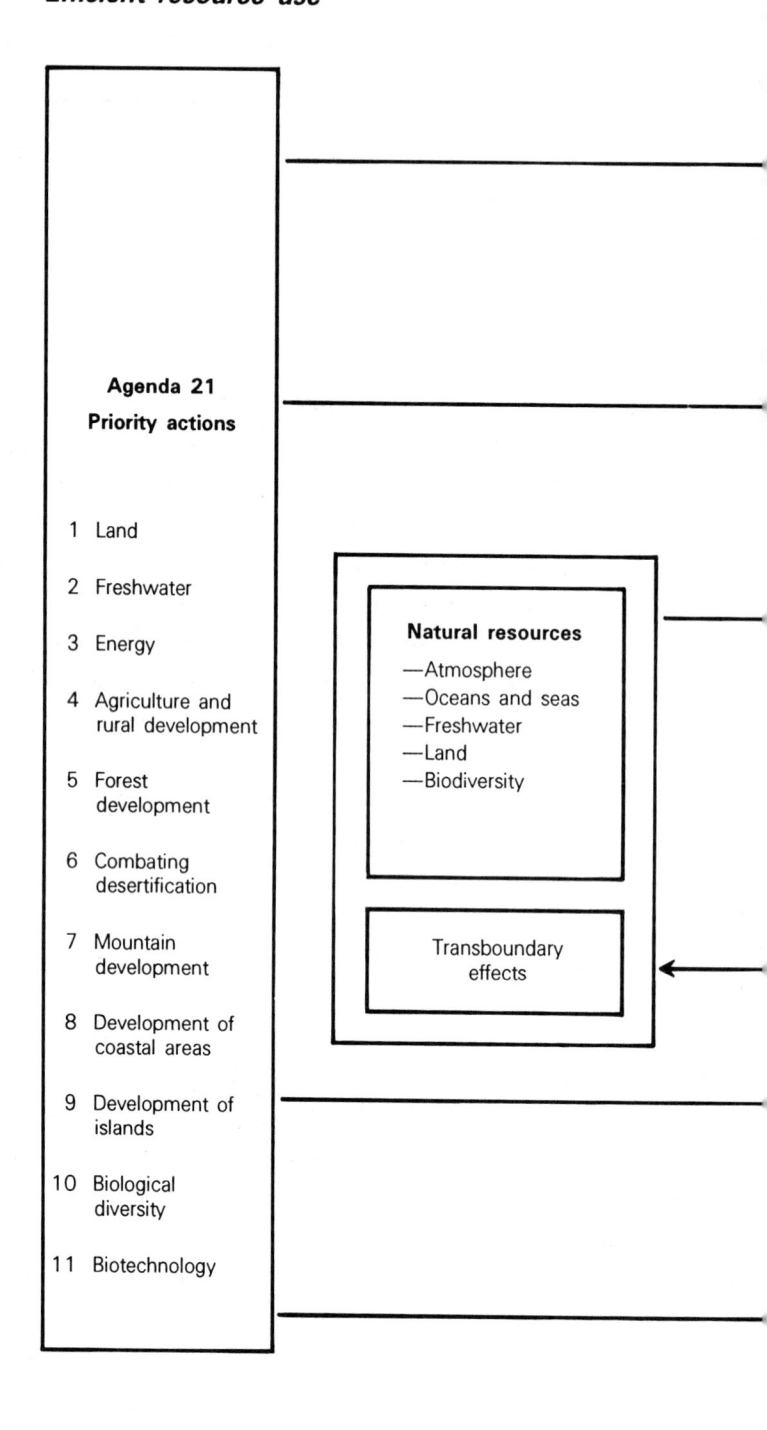

**Agenda 21
Priority actions**

1. Land
2. Freshwater
3. Energy
4. Agriculture and rural development
5. Forest development
6. Combating desertification
7. Mountain development
8. Development of coastal areas
9. Development of islands
10. Biological diversity
11. Biotechnology

Natural resources
— Atmosphere
— Oceans and seas
— Freshwater
— Land
— Biodiversity

Transboundary effects

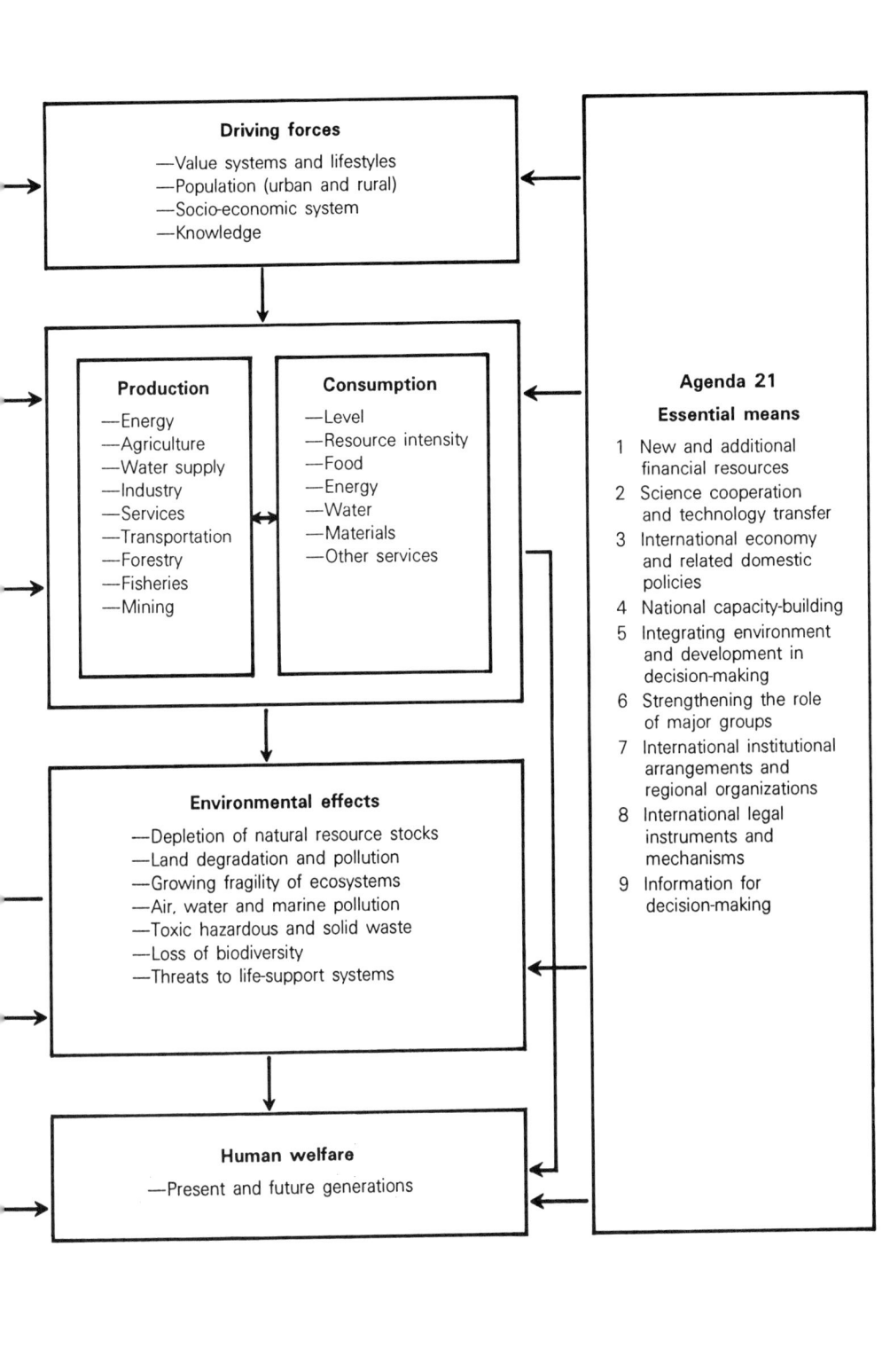

Driving forces
- Value systems and lifestyles
- Population (urban and rural)
- Socio-economic system
- Knowledge

Production
- Energy
- Agriculture
- Water supply
- Industry
- Services
- Transportation
- Forestry
- Fisheries
- Mining

Consumption
- Level
- Resource intensity
- Food
- Energy
- Water
- Materials
- Other services

Environmental effects
- Depletion of natural resource stocks
- Land degradation and pollution
- Growing fragility of ecosystems
- Air, water and marine pollution
- Toxic hazardous and solid waste
- Loss of biodiversity
- Threats to life-support systems

Human welfare
- Present and future generations

Agenda 21
Essential means
1. New and additional financial resources
2. Science cooperation and technology transfer
3. International economy and related domestic policies
4. National capacity-building
5. Integrating environment and development in decision-making
6. Strengthening the role of major groups
7. International institutional arrangements and regional organizations
8. International legal instruments and mechanisms
9. Information for decision-making

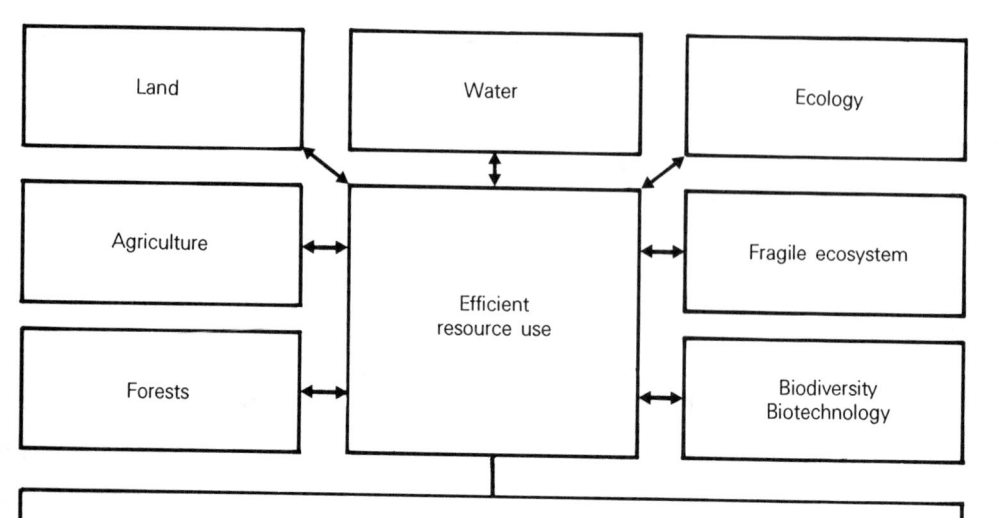

Efficient resource use

```
┌─────────────┐    ┌─────────────┐    ┌─────────────┐
│    Land     │    │    Water    │    │   Ecology   │
└─────────────┘    └─────────────┘    └─────────────┘
       ↘                 ↕                 ↙
┌─────────────┐    ┌─────────────┐    ┌─────────────────┐
│ Agriculture │←──→│             │←──→│ Fragile ecosystem│
└─────────────┘    │  Efficient  │    └─────────────────┘
                   │resource use │
┌─────────────┐    │             │    ┌─────────────────┐
│   Forests   │←──→│             │←──→│   Biodiversity  │
└─────────────┘    └─────────────┘    │  Biotechnology  │
                         │            └─────────────────┘
```

Cross-sectoral linkages

Accelerating sustainable development: International trade; adequate net financial flows; domestic policies (ch. 1.1)

Integration of environment and development in decision-making: Policy, planning and management level; economic instruments and marketing incentives; environmental accounting; legal and regulatory frameworks (ch. 1.2)

Combating poverty: Providing sustainable livelihoods (ch. 2.1)

Changing consumption patterns: Less wasteful lifestyles; sustainable consumption levels (ch. 2.2)

Demographic dynamics and sustainability: Global challenges; national and local level integration of population and environment (ch. 2.3)

Health: Pollution health risks; basic needs; communicable diseases; vulnerable groups (ch. 2.4)

Human settlements: Shelter; environmental infrastructure; energy and transport; disaster-prone areas (ch. 3.1)

Urban water supplies: Drinking water; sanitation (ch. 3.2)

Solid waste management: Waste minimization; safe disposal; recycling (ch. 3.3)

Urban pollution and health: Air pollution (ch. 3.4)

Atmosphere: Sustainable energy development and consumption; transport systems; industry; agriculture; ozone depletion; addressing uncertainties (ch. 5.1)

Oceans and seas: Marine protection; living resources; uncertainties and climate change (ch. 5.2)

Toxic chemicals: Chemical risks assessment; information; risks management programmes (ch. 6.1)

Hazardous wastes: Cleaner production; waste minimization; international cooperation for transboundary movement (ch. 6.2)

Radioactive wastes: International agreements for safe management (ch. 6.3)

Education, public awareness and training: (ch. 7.1)

Strengthening the role of major groups: Women; youth; indigenous people and their communities; NGOs; farmers; local authorities; trade unions; business and industry; scientific and technological community (ch. 7.2)

making a long-term transition to environmentally safe and sound energy systems.

Freshwater is a finite resource and, in many parts of the world, is becoming increasingly scarce. Also, deforestation, urbanization and poor farming and mining practices cause sedimentation in reservoirs; excessive use of agricultural chemicals, acid rain from industrial pollution, dumping of untreated sewage and factory wastes and over-pumping of ground water contribute to the deteriorating quality of water resources. An estimated 80 per cent of all diseases in developing countries, and one third of all deaths there, are related to contaminated water.

World food production—particularly in developing countries, where 80 per cent of the global population will live—should be doubled over the next four decades to meet the requirements of a rapidly growing population. The challenge is to apply the most efficacious methods of food production to high-potential lands, while drawing destructive agricultural practices away from marginal areas.

Forest resources are essential to both development and the preservation of the global environment. Mismanagement of forests is linked to degradation of soil and water, loss of wildlife and biological diversity, and pollution and global warming. Each year some 17 million hectares of tropical forests are lost as a result of agricultural and industrial expansion, overgrazing, excessive or poorly managed tree-cutting for fuel and similar human pressures. Air pollution and fires, in the meanwhile, are depleting the wooded lands in many developed countries. A holistic approach to forest conservation and development must address all relevant issues, including population pressures, unsustainable agricultural and industrial practices, land ownership, employment opportunities and external debt.

Desertification affects one fourth of the Earth's land area and one sixth of its people. To combat desertification, improved land and water use and reforestation are critical. Increased research and the provision of alternative livelihoods for subsistence farmers and herders are also needed, and more emphasis on preparing for drought emergencies is essential.

The rapid deterioration of mountain ecosystems threatens our planet's biological diversity and the well-being of people. Proposals should focus on halting erosion and replanting damaged areas, making natural disaster relief plans and offering alternative employment to people whose livelihoods are linked to harmful environmental practices.

Coastal and island settlements are threatened by human activities such as fishing, shipping, tourism, urban waste and pollution caused by industry, agriculture and forestry. Half of the world's population lives less than six kilometres away from the sea. By the year 2020, three fourths may reside in this coastal zone, which today includes many poor, densely crowded settlements. The well-being of people is closely related to the condition of fragile coastal environments. The environmentally destructive practices in coastal regions have to be curbed and damaged areas restored.

Sustaining the diversity of biological species—plant, animal and insect life—is a key element in the sustainable development of our planet. Short-term economic development today rarely considers the conservation of biological diversity (or biodiversity), and usually works against it. Present policies, both national and international, as well as market and accounting practices, discourage the sharing of benefits from this rich biodiversity: economic gain is often equated with resource depletion. Commitments to conserve biodiversity should be included in national development policies. This would involve policies on financing, technology transfer, debt, trade and environmental accounting.

Preserving the world's natural resources and biodiversity, and protecting the biosphere, while substantially increasing their productive yield, is one of civilization's greatest challenges. Halting and then reversing this environmental decline necessitates the mobilization of both progressive and valuable indigenous technologies. It requires relevant information and alternative approaches in the energy, agricultural, forestry and water sectors. It calls for increased awareness and training for more responsible resource use, and efforts to ensure that resource conservation does not threaten those who depend on these resources for their livelihood.

The global community should forge a partnership to halt the degradation of natural resources. It should use every means possible to reverse this degradation where feasible, and adopt sustainable practices for an early transition to efficient resource use. The critical need in the area of sustainable resource use is to adopt a policy approach that "anticipates and prevents", and it is only through such integrated, long-term and participatory policy planning and management strategies that a better quality of life can be assured for both present and future generations.

4.1 INTEGRATED APPROACH TO THE PLANNING AND MANAGEMENT OF LAND RESOURCES

Land is a physical entity as well as a system of natural resources. Land resources include soils, minerals, water and biota, which include microorganisms, plants and animals in all their biological and genetic diversity. All these elements interact to provide essential services, such as the recycling of wastes and materials, formation of soils, moderation of the water cycle and pollination of plants that maintain the productive capacity of the environment. These interactions form an important component of global cycles and geochemical processes and are closely linked to climate and other atmospheric phenomena. Land should always be regarded, first, as a set of terrestrial ecosystems, and not primarily as the inexhaustible supplier of resources.

Land provides much of the basic capital and resources on which development is founded. It satisfies primary human requirements for food, fibre and fuel, supplies many basic materials for industry and manufacturing, and provides space for human habitation and activities. Land also meets the needs of all other terrestrial species, whether wild or domestic. Hence, land resources are important for a vast array of human activities, from agriculture, forestry, water management and energy production to industry and construction, human settlements, communications infrastructure and waste disposal.

Since this finite resource cannot easily provide for rapidly increasing numbers of people and for a growing intensity of human activities, conflicts over land use are on the rise: among different social and economic interests, between humans and the environment and between immediate and long-term needs. Current management practices tend to view these needs in isolation from each other, as a result of which important links and impacts are ignored. Pressures on certain resources are leading to their deterioration and, eventually, to their permanent loss. In the past, traditional systems took account of the complexity of land and its diversity, and evolved effective management practices that conserved the resource base. These traditional systems, however, have not been able to cope with the sheer scale of modern activities. If development is to be sustainable, these conflicts over the use of land and its resources must be resolved. More effective practices should be developed to promote the ecological and economically efficient allocation of land resources, as well as the effective management of land resources and their socially equitable use.

An *integrated approach to the planning and management of land resources* is essential. Such a system should be able to deal with the broad issues but leave sufficient flexibility for decentralized resource management. It should be able to handle diversity and change, and satisfy the need for economic development and equity while protecting the environment and resource base that makes sustainable development possible. As a system, priorities can best be addressed through land use and physical planning; as a set of resources, land can best be managed through environmentally, socially and economically integrated practices.

Governments, in collaboration with appropriate local, national and international institutions and groups, should give immediate priority to promoting the most efficient use of land and its resources, and create mechanisms to facilitate active involvement by all parties concerned in decision-making regarding land and the use of its resources. Goals should be set and policies formulated to address the environmental, social and economic factors involved in land and land resource use. Out of this, policies should be enacted to encourage both the efficient use, protection and management of land and its resources and an improved distribution of population and activities according to the productivity of the land resource base. A general framework for land use and physical planning should be based on integrative units, such as the ecosystem or watershed, within which more specialized and sectoral plans can be developed. Improved planning and management systems would require the application of more appropriate tools for data collection and interpretation, as well as more accurate assessment and accounting of values, costs, benefits, risks and impacts.

4.2 PROTECTION OF THE QUALITY AND SUPPLY OF FRESHWATER RESOURCES: APPLICATION OF INTEGRATED APPROACHES TO THE DEVELOPMENT, MANAGEMENT AND USE OF WATER RESOURCES

Freshwater is a finite resource. It is indispensable for the sustenance of all life on Earth and is of vital importance to all socio-economic sectors as well. Human development would not be possible without the use of water sources. The multi-sectoral nature of water resources development, in the context of socio-economic growth, has to be recognized in addition to the multi-interest utilization of water resources for agriculture, industry, urban development, hydropower, inland fisheries, transportation, recreation and other activities. Rational water use schemes should be supported by simultaneous water conservation and wastage minimization measures, including the reuse of municipal sewage in agriculture and the recycling of industrial water.

Although it is indispensable, water is also a major carrier of disease and poses grave health problems in many developing countries. An estimated 80 per cent of all diseases and over one third of deaths in developing countries are caused by pathogen-loaded or disease vector-loaded water. Diseases caused by microbiological pollution of water supplies, transmitted by water-associated vectors or related to inadequate sanitation and absence of clean water are widespread. This problem is exacerbated by the rise in water consumption due to economic growth and population increase, resulting in greater volumes of sewage requiring treatment and disposal.

The widespread scarcity of freshwater resources, the progressive encroachment of incompatible activities and their gradual pollution and destruction in many world regions demand coordinated and integrated water resources development and management. Sound water resources development and management should view water as an integral part of the ecosystem, a natural resource and a social and economic good, the quantity and quality of which should determine its utilization. To this end, the availability and quality of water resources must be protected, with due consideration to its supply and the functioning of aquatic ecosystems, in order to satisfy water needs for human development activities.

To meet these needs, *integrated water resources development and management* are required to integrate technological, socio-economic, environmental and human health considerations into a dynamic, interactive, iterative and multi-sectoral approach to water resources management, including the identification and protection of potential sources of freshwater supply. Planning the rational utilization, protection, conservation and management of water resources should stem from community needs and priorities, fall within the framework of national economic development policy, and entail the full participation of the public, especially water-user groups and indigenous people and their communities. Water should be managed at the lowest appropriate level, involving district water committees and river catchment authorities. Also, appropriate institutional, legal and financial mechanisms should be established to ensure that water policy and its implementation become catalysts for sustainable development. Transboundary water resources and their use are of great importance to the riparian countries. Cooperation among these countries is desirable and legal agreements and other relevant arrangements may have to be made. Monitoring and data exchange to assess transboundary water resources are a first step toward harmonized management strategies.

At a global level, all nations should aim at the *protection of water resources, water quality and aquatic ecosystems* to identify potential sources of freshwater and prepare outlines for their protection, conservation and rational use. This is needed to implement enforceable standards for major point-source discharges and high-risk non-point sources. Countries should participate in international water quality monitoring and management programmes. Vector control programmes should also be pursued to reduce the prevalence of water-associated diseases. The effective protection of water resources and ecosystems from pollution requires considerable upgrading of most countries' present national capacities. Water quality management programmes require staffing and a minimum infrastructure to implement technical solutions, enforce regulatory actions, and maintain facilities.

The integrated management of water resources and liquid and solid wastes is a prerequisite for the provision of safe *drinking-water supply and sanitation.* Institutional reforms are needed to promote an integrated approach, including changes in procedures, attitudes and behaviour. This approach entails community management of services, backed by measures to strengthen local institutions in implementing and sustaining water and sanitation programmes. National capacities at all administrative levels, including institutional development, coordination, human resources, community participation, literacy and health and hygiene education must be built up. Institutional capacity-building must be given an equally high priority. Technical cooperation among developing countries in this area is important, especially in regard to the exchange of information and experience.

An international priority action programme on *water for sustainable food production and rural development* is relevant to assist developing countries in planning, developing and managing water resources on an integrated basis to meet present and future agricultural needs, taking into account environmental considerations such as irrigation potential. This priority programme should focus explicitly on water use efficiency, recycled waste water, small-scale irrigation schemes, waterlogging, salinity control and drainage in irrigated areas. Drinking-water supply and sanitation are a necessity for the unserved rural poor to prevent disabling diseases and to maintain their productive activities in the agricultural sector. Education in hygiene and cleanliness should be extended, and the participation of local communities—especially women and water users' groups—should be mobilized. A programme for the water management of inland fisheries and aquaculture should, as a priority, work to conserve water quality and quantity for optimum production and prevent aquacultural water pollution. This programme should also assist Member States in managing inland fisheries through the promotion of sustainable use and management as well as the development of environmentally sound means to intensify aquaculture. The importance of a functional and coherent institutional framework at the national level to promote water for sustainable agricultural development has been generally recognized. In addition, an adequate legal framework of rules and regulations should be in place to facilitate agricultural water use, drainage, water quality management and small-scale water development programmes, as well as the functioning of water users' and fishermen's associations. Legal measures that address the requirements of the agricultural water sector should stem from, and be consistent with, more general water resource management legislation.

The effective utilization and protection of freshwater resources require adequate funding. Recognizing the economic value of water, and stressing the satisfaction of basic needs, internal revenues should be generated for productive activities, reflecting marginal and opportunity costs. Funds should be obtained through cost recovery schemes, water tariffs, taxes and other means. Water resources development will require additional external support from multilateral or bilateral sources and the private sector.

Broad-based research and development programmes should help create, as well as field-test, innovative technologies and improved indigenous and traditional techniques in order to fully utilize and preserve limited water resources and safeguard them against pollution.

4.3 PROMOTING SUSTAINABLE AGRICULTURE AND RURAL DEVELOPMENT

Hunger and malnutrition are endemic in developing countries. By the year 2025, nearly 84 per cent of an estimated global population of 8.5 billion will be living in the developing countries. The fundamental challenge facing agriculture in the developing countries today is to increase food production in a sustainable way and feed expanding populations. Such an increase has to come primarily by intensifying current agricultural production, as the potential for bringing new land under cultivation in many countries is very limited. If hunger is to be eventually eradicated in these countries, this intensification must be both ecologically and socio-economically sustainable.

Agriculture is an important sector, if not the backbone, of the national economies of many developing countries, sometimes representing the major share of export earnings. Over the next 10 years, this sector will bear most of the responsibility for providing rural economies with sufficient growth to offer employment and other remunerative activities to the bulk of their population. Without this growth, the present rural-urban exodus is bound to accelerate, leading to unmanageable urban squalor and, in all likelihood, major socio-political upheavals. The need for sustainable off-farm rural development is, therefore, also critical.

Major adjustments are needed in national and international policies to create conditions for sustainable agriculture and rural development. A key objective is to increase food production in a sustainable way and raise household food security. This involves educational initiatives, economic incentives and the development of appropriate and new technologies, thereby ensuring stable supplies of adequate food by vulnerable groups, production for markets, employment and rural income generation, as well as efficient natural resources management and environmental protection. Priority should be given to maintaining and improving the capacity of higher potential agricultural lands to support an expanding population. At the same time, it is essential to conserve and rehabilitate lower potential land. Emphasis should also be placed on reforming agricultural policies relating to price, subsidies, trade, land tenure and appropriate farm practices and technologies.

In promoting sustainable agricultural and rural development, the commitment of national Governments and the support of the international community in implementing the programmes is crucial. Efficient agriculture will need to be job-creating, both on and off farm, and thus help reduce poverty levels. Major investments in rural infrastructure will be necessary.

The action programmes in Agenda 21 for agriculture and rural development combine basic development concern with sound environmental management. The first set of programmes deals with the effective halting of land degradation and the enrichment of soils. The problem of soil erosion is particularly acute in developing countries, where the productivity of vast areas of land is declining. Problems of salinization, waterlogging, soil pollution and loss of soil fertility are on the rise in all countries. In the meantime, populations are rapidly bugeoning, with an ever increasing demand for fuel, food and fibre. Long-term *land conservation and rehabilitation* programmes, with strong political support and adequate funding, and the participation of local communities, are essential to identify and implement effective conservation and rehabilitation measures to redress this serious threat.

An action programme on *land-resource planning information and education for agriculture* should be developed to systematically identify sustainable land use and production systems for each land and climate zone, control inappropriate land use, and take into account the actual potential and carrying capacities, as well as the limitation of land resources. Further, a set of actions on *sustainable plant nutrition to increase food production* would formulate strategies to maintain soil productivity. In many developing countries, where population growth exceeds agricultural production, the goal is to increase agricultural production substantially, particularly in high-potential areas, without destroying soil fertility. This will require determining and optimizing the use of organic fertilizer and other sources to enrich soil and thus increase farming efficiency and production.

Another key programme is *improving farm production and farming systems through diversification of farm and non-farm employment and infrastructure development*. Intensification should emphasize farm management technologies, such as crop rotation, organic manuring, the efficient and economically viable use of chemical inputs, agricultural waste recycling and the prevention of pre- and post-harvest losses. Where intensification is not possible, other employment opportunities, such as private small-scale agro-processing units, cottage industries, wildlife utilization, fisheries, conservation and reclamation activities and rural infrastructure should be created.

All countries need to comprehensively assess the impacts of macroeconomic policies and international trade relations on the performance of the food and agriculture sector and on food security. Actions towards an *agricultural policy review, planning and integrated programming in the light of the multifunctional aspect of agriculture, particularly with regard to food security and sustainable development*, are needed to integrate environmental considerations with sustainable agricultural development. National governments should also implement policies pertaining to land tenure, demographic trends, appropriate farm technologies and a more open trading system that would enhance access to food in rural households.

In the context of sustainable food and fibre crop production, there is an urgent need to safeguard the world's plant genetic resources. National and international action for the *conservation and sustainable utilization of plant genetic resources for food and sustainable agriculture* should place special emphasis on endogenous capacity for plant characterization, evaluation and use. Measures should be taken to strengthen networks of *in situ* conservation areas and improve the tools for *ex situ* collections. Similarly, action for the *conservation and sustainable utilization of animal genetic resources for sustainable agriculture* are important to increase the quantity and quality of animal products and conserve the existing diversity of animal breeds to meet future requirements. Certain local animal breeds have unique attributes for adaptation, disease resistance and specific uses, in addition to their sociocultural value, and should be preserved.

Between 25 per cent and 50 per cent of pre- and post-harvest losses are estimated to be caused by pests. Pests affecting animal health also cause heavy losses and, in many areas, prevent livestock development. Chemical control of agricultural pests has dominated the scene, but its overuse has had adverse effects on farm budgets, human health and the environment, and new pest problems continue to develop. *Integrated pest management and control in agriculture*, which combines a variety of biological, cultural and chemical as well as host-plant resistance and appropriate farming practices, should minimize the use of pesticides. Placing the components of such a strategy within the economic reach of the farmer guarantees yields, reduces costs, and is environmentally friendly. Integrated pest management should go hand in hand with appropriate pesticide management to allow for pesticide regulation and control, including trade, and for the safe handling and disposal of pesticides, particularly those that are toxic.

Programmes on *rural energy transition to enhance productivity* would increase energy inputs available in these areas for human productivity and income generation. Energy supplies in many countries are not commensurate with their development needs. In the rural areas of developing countries, the chief sources of energy are fuelwood, crop residues and manure, together with animal and human energy. The programme on rural energy transition would initiate a process in rural communities from informal energy sources, such as fuelwood, to structured and diversified sources, by making available new and renewable alternative sources of energy.

The participation of local people and communities is crucial for the success of sustainable agriculture. The activities under the programme *ensuring people's participation and promoting human resource development for sustainable agriculture* will strengthen the capacity of rural institutions, extension services, and decentralized decision making, which will enhance control over local natural resources. It also works to guarantee the equitable access of rural people, particularly women, to land, water and other natural resources, as well as to technologies and financing.

The increase of solar ultraviolet radiation due to the depletion of the ozone layer has been recorded in various parts of the world, in particular in the southern hemisphere. Action needs to be taken for the *evaluation of the effects of ultraviolet radiation on plants and animals caused by the depletion of the stratospheric ozone layer* and take appropriate remedial measures.

4.4 COMBATING DEFORESTATION

Increasing attention is being given to the condition of the world's forests and to the role they play in local economies, and in the quality of life. Public concern has focused for several years on tropical forests. It is now, however, clearly accepted that all types of forests should be taken into account. Recent estimates indicate that annual deforestation rates of tropical forests amount to some 17 million hectares worldwide. Little is known on the overall situation of forests—boreal, sustral, subtemperate and temperate—and on their exact quantity, quality and rates of change. Deforestation is a result of many causes. Some are natural, but many are due to human interference for development purposes, including inappropriate land tenure systems and incentives, expansion of agricultural areas, increasing forest product demand and lack of information and understanding on the value of forests.

In the context of environmentally sound and sustainable development, the benefits to be derived from trees, forests and forest lands are wide and varied. Forests are not only sources of timber and firewood, but also play an important role in soil conservation, the regulation of hydrological cycles, exchange of gases and nutrients, including carbon dioxide, and the maintenance of reservoirs of rich biodiversity. Many local populations have understood the multiple benefits for their livelihoods obtained from forests, yet only recently has the fundamental value of forests emerged on a wider national and global scale. The realization that forests significantly affect the lives of both local and distant populations has helped place forest-related issues on national planning and on the international agenda.

Maintaining and increasing forest cover will contribute to improved human living conditions and the preservation of biodiversity, particularly through environmentally sound land management practices. While preserving primary forest areas is critical for biodiversity protection, planting new forests will significantly contribute to timber and firewood production, protect watersheds and soil, function as carbon sinks and in general release the pressure of exploitation on remaining primary forests.

Agenda 21 includes a series of urgent action programmes for the development and conservation of forest resources. In a programme for the sustainable development of forests and woodlands, the first priority is in *sustaining the multiple roles and functions of all types of forests, forest lands and woodlands* by strengthening national institutions and capabilities to formulate and implement effectively policies, plans, programmes and projects relevant to forest issues. The scope and effectiveness of conservation and forest expansion activities should be enhanced, and the sustainable production of forest goods and services in both developed and developing countries should be ensured.

Preventive measures are required for *enhancing the protection, sustainable management and conservation of all forests, and the greening of degraded areas, through forest rehabilitation, afforestation, reforestation and other rehabilitative means.* These priority activities should work to conserve and sustainably manage existing and new forest resources, increasing their ecological, biological, climatic, sociocultural and economic contributions while preserving their biodiversity.

Another group of priority activities should aim at *promoting efficient utilization and assessment to recover the full valuation of the goods and services provided by forests, forest lands and woodlands* and ensuring their sustainable management in a manner consistent with land use, environmental considerations and development needs. It should also work towards the more efficient and rational use of trees and forest resources, including the development of forest-based processing industries, value-adding secondary processing and trade in forest products.

The strengthening of existing systems and the establishment of new ones for *establishing and/or strengthening capacities for the planning, assessment and systematic observa-*

tion of forests and related programmes, projects and activities, including commercial trade and processes, should focus on the impacts of programmes, projects and activities on the quality and extent of forest resources, the land available for afforestation, and land tenure. These systems should be integrated in a continuous process of research, coordinated data and accessible information and in-depth research analysis, while ensuring necessary modifications and improvements in the planning and decision-making process.

Forests play a critical role in global environment and development issues and warrant international coordinated efforts to develop response strategies. International cooperation, particularly at the regional level, can address specific issues that national activities are sometimes not equipped to do. Whereas a relatively small forest might not warrant a large national investment programme on the climatic regulatory function of forests, such a globally relevant activity might have a great value internationally. International and regional cooperation is required to ensure the development of local capacity and to strengthen the local organizations responsible for forest conservation and sustainable management.

Of particular importance is the need for the international community to support the implementation of the non-legally binding Forest Principles on the management, conservation and sustainable development of all types of forests. These Principles address all types of forests, both natural or planted in all geographic regions and climatic zones, while recognizing that the subject of forests is related to the entire range of environmental and developmental issues and opportunities, including socio-economic development. They underline the need for timely, reliable and accurate information on forests and forest ecosystems and the need for participation of interested parties, such as local communities, women, youth, industries and labour. The principles also insist on the sovereign rights of States to exploit their resources pursuant to their own environmental policies.

On the basis of the implementation of the Forest Principles approved at the Rio Conference in June of 1992, consideration should be given to the need and feasibility of appropriate internationally agreed arrangements to promote international cooperation.

4.5 MANAGING FRAGILE ECOSYSTEMS

Strategies for sustainable development in Agenda 21 specifically address the problems of fragile ecosystems and the pressing need to reverse the destruction of renewable resources, as well as programmes for the sustainable use of land, freshwater, and biological and genetic resources.

There are fragile—and important—ecosystems in deserts, semi-arid lands, mountains, wetlands, small islands and certain coastal areas, possessing unique features and resources. Most of these ecosystems are regional in scope, as they transcend national boundaries. Other major ecosystems, such as mountains, are important sources of water, energy and biological diversity, and provide minerals, forest and agricultural products, as well as recreation. They also represent the complex and interrelated ecology of our planet.

The central thrust of the Agenda 21 action programmes here is to incorporate the multi-sectoral nature of land, water, energy and biotic resource growth into socio-economic development and the multi-interest use of these resources for agriculture, forestry, industry, urban development, inland fisheries, transportation, recreation and other activities.

The core challenge here is to raise productivity and incomes, especially of the poor, and without irreversibly degrading and depleting critical life support systems in such fragile environments. This must be done in a manner that raises productivity and meets rising human demands while ensuring the sustainable management of fragile ecosystems.

4.5.1 *Managing fragile ecosystems: combating desertification and drought*

Desertification is land degradation in arid, semi-arid and dry sub-humid areas, caused by many factors, including climatic variations and human activities. It affects about 1 billion people and one quarter of the total land area of the world. Desertification is most severe in the world's drylands, amounting to about 3.6 billion hectares. The decline in productivity and loss of crop and livestock production in these areas has resulted in widespread poverty, hunger and malnutrition.

In combating desertification and drought, national Governments and the international community should aim at *strengthening the knowledge base and developing information and monitoring systems for regions prone to desertification and drought, including the economic and social aspects of these ecosystems*. Global assessments of the status and rate of desertification should take into account the socio-economic causes and their interactions with climatic cycles and drought. Adequate world-wide systematic observation systems are helpful for the development and implementation of effective anti-desertification programmes. An integrated and coordinated information and systematic observation system based on appropriate technology and embracing global, regional, national and local levels is essential for understanding the dynamics of desertification and drought processes.

In *combating land degradation through, inter alia, intensified soil conservation, afforestation and reforestation activities*, preventive measures should be launched in areas which are not yet affected or are only slightly affected by desertification; corrective measures should be implemented to sustain the productivity of moderately desertified land; and rehabilitative measures should be taken to recover severely or very severely desertified drylands.

There is an urgent need for *developing and strengthening integrated development programmes for the eradication of poverty and promotion of alternative livelihood systems in areas prone to desertification*. Current livelihood and resource use systems cannot provide adequate living standards in these fragile areas where there is drought and increasing population pressure. Poverty has to a major extent accelerated the rate of environmental degradation and desertification. Action is needed to rehabilitate and improve subsistence agriculture and agro-pastoral systems for sustainable management of rangelands as well as the promotion of alternative livelihood systems.

Developing comprehensive anti-desertification programmes and integrating them into national development plans and national environmental planning is essential. In a number of developing countries, the natural resource base subject to desertification is the main resource on which development depends. The social systems interacting with land resources make the problem much more complex and necessitate an integrated land planning and management approach. Proposals for strengthening international cooperation in the fight against desertification through the preparation of an international convention to combat desertification in all affected areas of the world, particularly in Africa, were endorsed at the Earth Summit. It is expected that this convention will be finalized by June of 1994.

Efforts should also include *developing comprehensive drought preparedness and drought-relief schemes, including self-help arrangements, for drought-prone areas and designing programmes to cope with environmental refugees*. Drought, in differing degrees of frequency and severity, is a recurring problem throughout much of the developing world, particularly in Africa. Apart from the toll on human lives, the economic costs of drought-related disasters are high, due to lost production and diversion of scarce development resources. Early-warning systems which forecast drought will make possible the implementation of drought-preparedness schemes. Integrated programmes at local levels, such as alternative cropping strategies, soil and water conservation, and the promotion of water-harvesting techniques, would reduce the impacts of drought while providing basic necessities.

Encouraging and promoting popular participation and environmental education, focusing on desertification control and management of the effects of drought is also crucial. The experience to date as to whether projects and programmes related to desertification and drought control succeed or fail points to the need to focus on obtaining popular involvement rooted in the concept of partnership and the sharing of responsibilities by all parties.

4.5.2 *Managing fragile ecosystems: sustainable mountain development*

Mountain ecosystems are an important source of biological diversity, water and mineral resources. Forestry, agriculture and recreation form important economic activities in many mountain areas. The ability of mountain ecosystems to continue contributing to human development is, however, diminishing due to a variety of natural and human factors. Mountain ecosystems are susceptible to accelerated soil erosion, landslides and the rapid loss of habitat and genetic diversity. About 10 per cent of the Earth's population live in mountain areas with higher slopes, while some 40 per cent occupy the adjacent medium- and low-watershed regions. In many mountain areas, natural resources degradation is causing widespread poverty among local inhabitants. The proper management of mountain resources and socio-economic development deserves high priority.

Mountain habitats have a rich variety of ecosystems. A single mountain slope may include tropical, subtropical, and temperate climates, each representing microcosms of habitat diversity. The conservation and sustainable development of mountain resources requires, as a priority, *generating and strengthening knowledge about the ecology and sustainable development of mountain ecosystems*, and *promoting integrated watershed development and alternative livelihood opportunities*.

Specific information on the ecology, natural resource potential and socio-economic activities of mountain ecosystems is essential. Undertaking surveys on soils, forests, water use and crop, plant and animal resources to facilitate the integrated management and environmental assessment of mountain ecosystems is essential. Providing incentives to local people for the use and transfer of environmentally friendly technologies, improved farming and conservation practices, integrating forest, rangelands and wildlife activities, establishing reserves in species-rich areas, and tourism in accordance with the proper management of the area are among the key activities in the sustainable development of mountain ecosystems.

Existing institutions at national, regional and local levels should be strengthened to generate a multidisciplinary land/water ecological knowledge base on mountain ecosystems and identify hazardous areas that are most vulnerable to erosion, floods and landslides. This would require the establishment of meteorological and hydrological monitoring systems.

Promoting integrated watershed development and alternative livelihood opportunities is central to sustainable mountain development. The serious ecological deterioration in watershed areas is largely due to poor land management practices and cultivation of marginal lands. Soil erosion is devastating, and there is widespread poverty in these areas. Integrated watershed development programmes should be implemented to prevent further ecological imbalances. An integrated approach would link the natural resource capital of plant and animal species and water and land with human resources, for their conservation and sustainable use. A major objective of such priority programmes should be to develop alternative livelihood opportunities, particularly through employment schemes, that would maximize the productive base.

To prevent soil erosion, increase biomass production and maintain the ecological balance, priority activities directed towards integrated watershed development should aim at developing appropriate land-use systems for both arable and non-arable land in mountain areas. They should also promote alternative income-generating activities and improve infrastructure and social services. Technical assistance and institutional arrangements would be required to help mitigate the effects of natural disasters in mountain areas through hazard-prevention measures, risk zoning, early warning systems, evacuation plans and emergency supplies.

4.5.3 Managing fragile ecosystems: integrated management and sustainable development of coastal areas, including exclusive economic zones

Coastal zones, the interface between land and sea, are not simply transition areas. They contain highly diverse ecosystems and some of the world's most biologically productive habitats. Uses of coastal space are multiple and include settlement, food production, derivation of energy, minerals and other raw materials, tourism, recreation and transport. Coastal zone boundaries are defined by political, administrative and ecological considerations.

More than 60 per cent of the global population lives within 60 kilometres of a shoreline. By the year 2020, this figure could rise to nearly three quarters of the world's population. Two thirds of the world's cities with populations of 2.5 million or more are near tidal estuaries. Many of the world's poor are crowded into coastal areas and, consequently, coastal resources are vital for many local communities and indigenous people. The Exclusive Economic Zone (EEZ) is important for the development and protection of natural resources, both for coastal countries and—especially—for small island developing States.

Coastal zones, in a sense, act as the "sink" of the continents, in that their degradation and pollution have both local and distant inland sources. Inadequate tenure systems, bad land-use practices, fertilization, pest control, poor watershed management, clearance of forests on steep lands, industrial pollution and the expansion of human settlements, ports and recreational areas have all contributed. Despite national, subregional, regional and international levels, the current sectoral and disciplinary approach to marine and coastal development does not provide an effective framework for achieving sustainability and resolving conflicts over resource use. In the meantime, the coastal environment continues to be rapidly degraded and eroded in many parts of the world.

The current patterns of coastal areas management reflect historical conditions which are no longer valid. In the past, for instance, there were smaller coastal populations with less advanced fishing technologies, and the supply of ocean and coastal resources was as a result not constraining. Today, however, the demand for fisheries is high and policies on uses of coastal and ocean environments are creating conflicts among users, as well as significant resource depletion and environmental degradation. A perspective on integrated coastal management must recognize the need for proactive and anticipatory regimes that prevent environmental damage and promote economic growth while ensuring the equitable allocation of user rights. The scales of resource management and economic regimes must, therefore, be adjusted to meet the ecologically sustainable development needs of coastal countries and island States. This requires a holistic and integrated management approach that fully evaluates the coastal resource base and its opportunities and constraints.

The central priority is to develop guidelines for the *integrated management and sustainable development of coastal areas, including exclusive economic zones*. This is particularly important in regard to fragile interrelated ecosystems such as those found in small island developing States, low-lying countries and enclosed and semi-enclosed seas. An appropriate policy and legal framework for land-use and siting policies should be formulated that would regulate management and rates of use, promote environmentally sound technology and sustainable practices, make environmental impact assessments mandatory, and develop technologies and endogenous scientific and technological capabilities. Coastal profiles should be developed to identify critical areas, patterns of management and user conflicts. Contingency plans should be prepared to deal with sewage treatment and potential natural disasters, including potential sea level rise due to modifications in the climate, and restore altered critical habitats. At the national level, coordinating mechanisms should be established to ensure participation of the academic and private sectors, non-governmental organizations, women, youth, indigenous people and local user groups in every aspect of government planning. Centres of excellence and programmes for pilot demonstration and human resource development should be supported.

4.5.4 *Managing fragile ecosystems: sustainable development of small islands*

Small island developing States and islands supporting small communities are a special case for environment and development. They are ecologically fragile and vulnerable. They have a high share of global biodiversity. Their small size, limited resources, geographic dispersion and isolation from markets places them at an economic disadvantage and prevents economies of scale. For small island developing States, the ocean and coastal environment is of strategic importance and constitutes a valuable development resource.

The economic growth of many small island developing States depends on the marine resources in waters within their national jurisdiction and on the high seas. Given the potential threats of global climate change and sea level rise, some States could, over the long term, be threatened with the loss of their entire territories.

The sparse scale of small island developing States places inherent limits on their total developmental capacity. Existing capacity must, therefore, be restructured to cope efficiently with the needs of sustainable development and integrated management within the given human and financial means. New technologies should be used to increase the capacity of tiny populations to meet their requirements.

In view of their limited capacity and financial means, the *sustainable development of small islands* should involve the adoption and implementation of sustainable development plans, including meeting essential human needs within island limits, maintaining biodiversity and increasing the quality of life for island peoples. To this end, small island developing States, with the appropriate assistance of international and regional organizations, should prepare medium- and long-term plans for sustainable development that integrate the multiple uses of limited resources and identify types of development compatible with their limits. This would involve adapting coastal area management techniques to the special characteristics of islands, making inventories of natural resources and species and defining measures to protect endangered species and maintain biodiversity.

Measures should be adopted to cope with environmental change, mitigate impacts and lessen threats to marine and coastal resources. In addition, the overall carrying capacity of small island developing States should be assessed under different development assumptions and resource constraints. The vulnerability and response options of small island developing States to global change and potential sea level rise should be evaluated. Response strategies, based on the anticipate-and-prevent principle, should be formulated, addressing the environmental, social and economic effects of climate change and sea level rise, and appropriate contingency plans should be readied.

4.6 CONSERVATION OF BIOLOGICAL DIVERSITY

Biological diversity—or "biodiversity"—is the expression which has been coined to describe the variety of the genes, species and ecosystems found on our planet. It embraces all life forms, from plant and animal life to micro-organisms and the water, land and air in which they live and interact. This richness—the Earth's living wealth—provides an abundant and essential supply of indispensable goods and services. Biological resources feed and clothe us and provide housing, medicines and spiritual nourishment, among other basic needs. Human well-being and development are thus heavily reliant on biodiversity and its components.

Although only about 1.4 million species have been described, it has been estimated that there are at least 5 million and perhaps as many as 100 million species on Earth. Most of these are found in the natural ecosystems of forests, savannas, pastures and rangelands, deserts, tundra, rivers, lakes and seas. Farmers' fields and gardens are also of great importance as repositories, while gene banks, botanical gardens, zoos and other germplasm repositories make small but significant contributions.

The current decline in the world's biodiversity is largely the result of human activities, resulting in habitat destruction, over-harvesting, pollution and the inappropriate introduction of foreign plants and animals. Although the full consequences of this loss of biodiversity are unknown, there are, nevertheless, compelling scientific, ethical and socio-economic reasons for conserving the many life forms on Earth. Biological resources constitute a capital asset with great potential for yielding sustainable benefits, with new ways constantly being found in which they can contribute to sustainable development through, for example, more nutritional foods, new and improved pharmaceuticals and many other products.

Urgent and decisive action is needed to conserve and maintain genes, species and ecosystems, with a view to the sustainable management and use of biological resources. Capacities for the assessment, study and systematic observation and evaluation of biodiversity need to be reinforced at national and international levels. Effective national action and international cooperation are required for the *in situ* protection of ecosystems, for the *ex situ* conservation of biological and genetic resources and for the enhancement of ecosystem functions. The participation and support of local communities are essential to the success of such an approach. Recent advances in biotechnology have pointed to the potential use of the genetic material contained in plants, animals and micro-organisms for agricultural, agro-forestry, health and welfare and environmental purposes.

The aims of the programme for the *conservation of biological diversity* include pressing for the early entry into force of the Convention on Biological Diversity with the widest possible participation, the development of national strategies for the conservation of biological diversity and the sustainable use of biological resources, and the integration of such strategies into national development strategies and/or plans. The implementation of measures for sharing the benefits derived from the research and development and use of biological and genetic resources, the carrying out of country studies, and the production of regular world reports on biodiversity based upon national assessments are further key elements in this programme. In addition, the recognition and fostering of traditional methods and the knowledge of indigenous people and their communities, the implementation of mechanisms for the improvement, generation, development and sustainable use of biotechnology and its safe transfer, and the promotion of broader international and regional cooperation are critical to furthering scientific and economic understanding of the importance of biodiversity and its functions.

4.7 ENVIRONMENTALLY SOUND MANAGEMENT OF BIOTECHNOLOGY

Biotechnology is the integration of new techniques emerging from modern biotechnology with the well-established approaches of traditional biotechnology. It is a set of enabling techniques for bringing about specific changes in genetic material in plants, animals and microbial systems leading to useful products and technology. By itself, biotechnology cannot resolve all the fundamental problems of environment and development, and expectations need to be tempered by realism. Nevertheless, it promises to make a significant contribution to sustainable development, through better health care, enhanced food security through sustainable agricultural practices, improved supplies of potable water, more efficient industrial development processes, support for sustainable methods of afforestation and reforestation and the detoxification of hazardous wastes. Biotechnology also offers new opportunities for global partnerships, particularly between those countries that are rich in biological resources but lacking the necessary expertise and investments to apply such resources through biotechnology, and those that have developed the technological expertise to transform biological resources to serve the needs of sustainable development.

Five programme areas have been developed which seek to foster internationally agreed principles to be applied to ensure the environmentally sound management of biotechnology, to engender public trust and confidence, to promote the development of sustainable applications of biotechnology and to establish appropriate enabling mechanisms, especially within developing countries.

The first programme area focuses upon the need for *increasing the availability of food, feed and renewable raw materials*. The challenge is to increase food production to meet the accelerating demands of a growing world-wide population through the successful and environmentally safe application of biotechnology in agriculture. It is proposed to apply biotechnology to increase to the optimum possible extent the yield of major crops, livestock and aquaculture species, to reduce the need for volume increases of food, feed and raw materials by improving the nutritional value of the source crops, animals and micro-organisms, to increase the use of integrated pest, disease and crop management techniques, to eliminate overdependence on agro-chemicals, to evaluate the agricultural potential of marginal lands, to expand the applications of biotechnology in forestry, to increase the efficiency of nitrogen fixation and mineral absorption in higher plants and to improve basic and applied science capabilities.

The second programme area focuses upon *improving human health*. Increasing environmental degradation, along with poor and inadequate development, continue to take a heavy toll on human health. New and improved medicines and other pharmaceutical products have an increasingly important contribution to make in tackling the causes of poor health. The aim is to contribute to an overall health programme, to reinforce or inaugurate programmes to help combat major communicable diseases, as well as to promote good general health among people of all ages, to develop and improve programmes for major non-communicable diseases, to develop appropriate safety procedures and to enhance research capacities.

The third programme area is aimed at *enhancing the protection of the environment*. Poor land and waste management and increasing use of chemicals, energy and other resources by an expanding global population have all led to major environmental problems. Biotechnology is one of many tools which can help the rehabilitation of degraded ecosystems and landscapes through the development of new techniques for reforestation and afforestation, germplasm conservation and cultivation of new plant varieties suitable for fragile environments. The programme area calls for the adoption of production processes making optimal use of natural resources, the promotion of the use of biotechnologies for the bio-remediation of land and water, waste treatment, soil conservation, reforestation and afforestation and land rehabilitation, and the application of biotechnologies and their products with a view to long-term ecological security.

Integral to the application of biotechnology is a programme area for *enhancing safety and developing international mechanisms for cooperation*. This is aimed at ensuring safety in biotechnology development, application, exchange and transfer through international agreement on principles to be applied on risk assessment and management, with particular reference to health and environmental considerations, including the widest possible public participation, and taking into account ethical considerations. Only when adequate and transparent safety and border-control procedures are in place will the community at large be able to derive maximum benefit from, and be in a much better position to accept the potential benefits and risks of, biotechnology. Among other activities, it has been agreed to compile, update and develop compatible safety procedures into a framework of internationally agreed principles as a basis for guidelines to be applied on safety in biotechnology, including consideration of the need for, and feasibility of, an international agreement, and to promote information exchange as a basis for further development, drawing on the work already undertaken by international or other expert bodies.

The final programme area is aimed at *establishing enabling mechanisms for the development and the environmentally sound application of biotechnology.* Institutional capacities need to be strengthened at the national and regional levels to accelerate the development and application of biotechnologies, particularly in developing countries. These need to be coupled with efforts to enhance enabling factors such as training capacity, know-how, research and development facilities and funds, industrial building capacity, capital (including venture capital), protection of intellectual property rights and expertise in areas such as developing countries. This programme area aims to enhance existing efforts at national, regional and global levels to: provide the necessary support for research and product development; raise public awareness of the benefits and risks of biotechnology; help create a favourable climate for investments, industrial capacity-building and distribution/marketing; encourage international exchanges of scientists, to discourage the "brain drain"; and foster the traditional methods and knowledge of indigenous people and their local communities and enable them to participate in any benefits arising from developments in biotechnology. Among other activities it has been agreed to undertake an urgent review of existing enabling mechanisms, programmes and activities at the national, regional and global levels to identify strengths, weaknesses and gaps, and to assess the priority needs of developing countries.

5

GLOBAL AND REGIONAL RESOURCES

THE sustainable management of our planet's global and transboundary resources—comprising its atmosphere, oceans and seas, as well as its living marine resource—is in the interest of all of Earth's inhabitants. Environmental changes affect and influence the very survival of our planet: the way in which human activities bear on the global and regional resources are multitudinous and complex, and their severity is beyond question.

Two events underscored this problem early in 1992. The depletion of the stratospheric ozone over the northern latitudes was found to have created a hole in the atmosphere similar to the one discovered over Antarctica. At the same time, the largest city in the world was partially shut down by air pollution that reached hazardous levels. Climate change is perhaps the most intractable threat to human well-being and the survival of many of the species on Earth. Industrialized countries are responsible for most greenhouse gas emissions; yet it is the developing countries which are most likely to bear the brunt of the effects of climate change. Increased support to developing countries will be needed to enable them to respond to climate change and to take less polluting paths on their road to economic growth.

Though its full consequences are uncertain, atmospheric pollution, and the consequent threat of greenhouse warming, is a major concern of the international community today, both due to its potential impact on human welfare and its profound implications for precautionary measures and policy-making, particularly energy policy. Even a small rise in the Earth's sea level could have disastrous consequences, particularly upon islands and low-lying coastal areas. The pollution of the world's coastal areas, oceans and seas and the overexploitation of their living marine resources spoil their enormous productive potential and threaten the populations dependent on the sea for their sustenance and livelihoods.

Overfishing and the degradation of marine habitats throughout the world are depleting a major food resource. Steps should be taken to maintain fish populations at sustainable levels. National licensing programmes should be used to allocate access to fish resources equitably among commercial and recreational fishers, respecting the rights of community-based groups and indigenous peoples and their communities. Developing countries need assistance to promote deep-sea fishing to reduce the use of coastal fisheries.

These global and regional problems present a formidable challenge: all nations must unite in cooperation and commitment if efforts are to succeed. The cause of these problems, many of them indirect, are highly interwoven into production processes and consumption patterns. They require us to act outside of the normal time scales of political and economic decision-making on evidence that is compelling but incomplete and, in some important cases, even controversial. They will also require considerable monitoring and information-gathering activities on global and local levels. The sustainable management of these common resources will inevitably affect

Global and regional resources

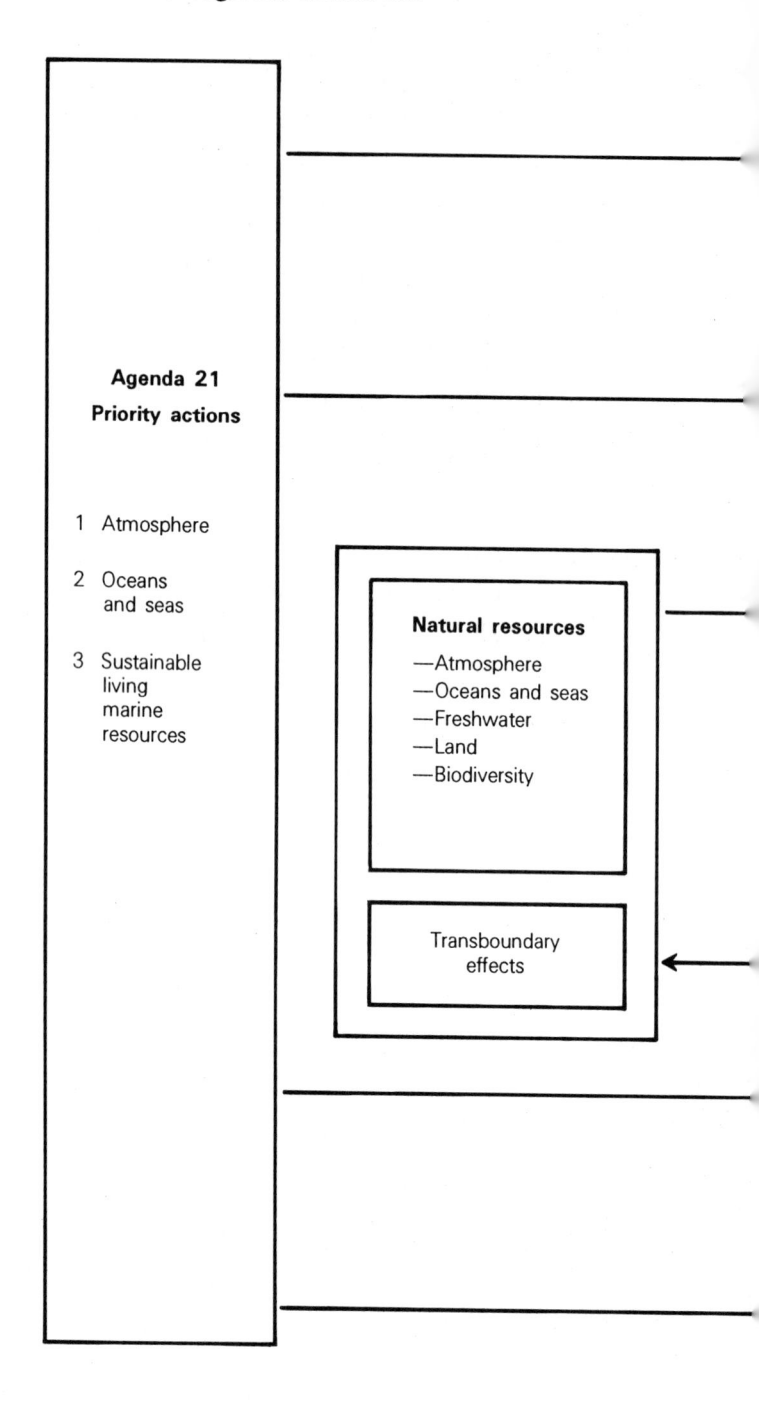

Agenda 21
Priority actions

1 Atmosphere

2 Oceans
  and seas

3 Sustainable
  living
  marine
  resources

Natural resources
—Atmosphere
—Oceans and seas
—Freshwater
—Land
—Biodiversity

Transboundary
effects

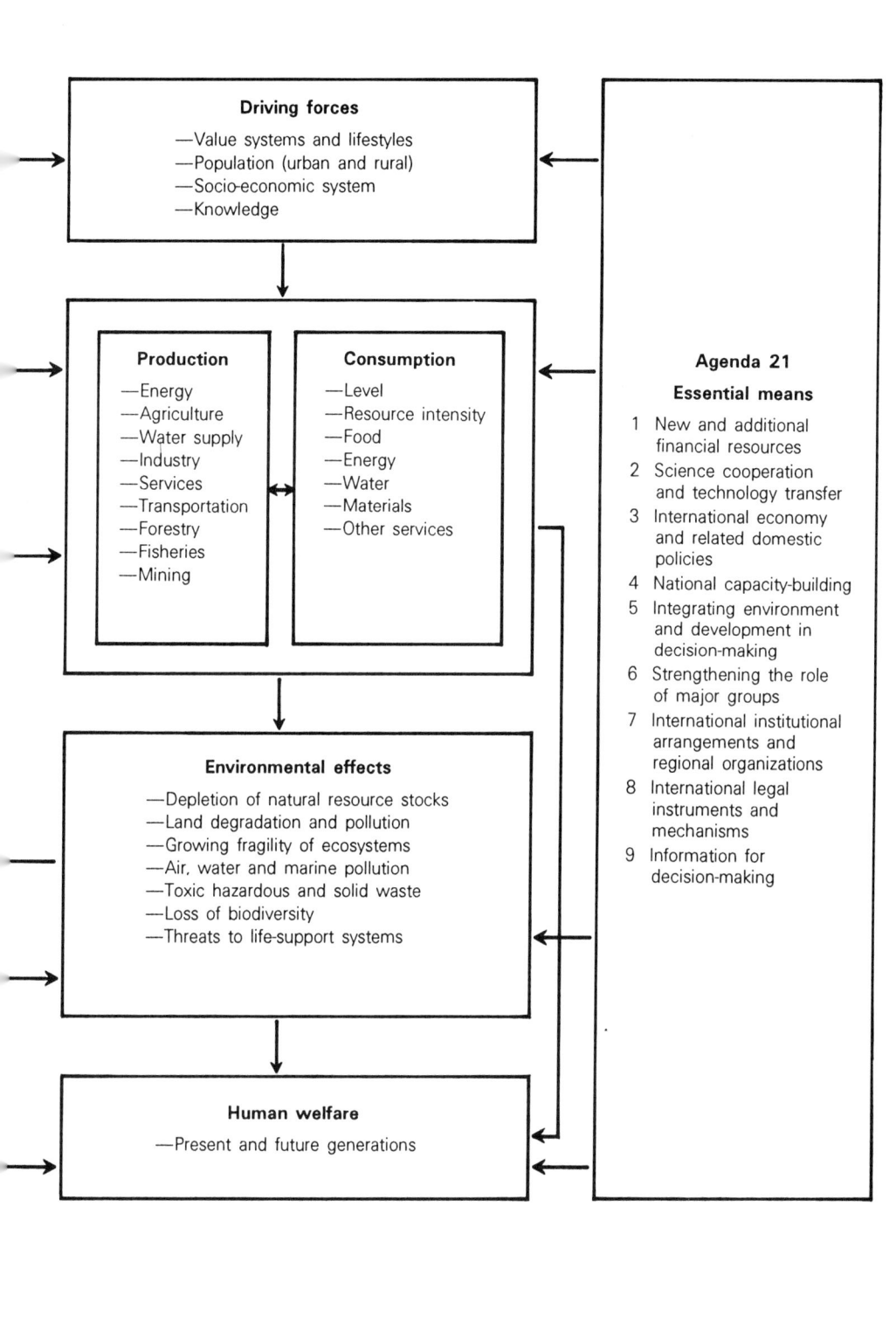

Driving forces
- Value systems and lifestyles
- Population (urban and rural)
- Socio-economic system
- Knowledge

Production
- Energy
- Agriculture
- Water supply
- Industry
- Services
- Transportation
- Forestry
- Fisheries
- Mining

Consumption
- Level
- Resource intensity
- Food
- Energy
- Water
- Materials
- Other services

Agenda 21
Essential means
1. New and additional financial resources
2. Science cooperation and technology transfer
3. International economy and related domestic policies
4. National capacity-building
5. Integrating environment and development in decision-making
6. Strengthening the role of major groups
7. International institutional arrangements and regional organizations
8. International legal instruments and mechanisms
9. Information for decision-making

Environmental effects
- Depletion of natural resource stocks
- Land degradation and pollution
- Growing fragility of ecosystems
- Air, water and marine pollution
- Toxic hazardous and solid waste
- Loss of biodiversity
- Threats to life-support systems

Human welfare
- Present and future generations

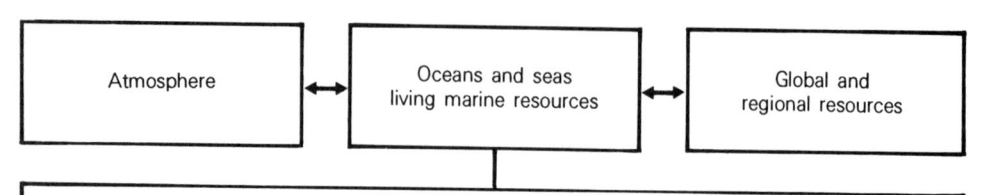

Global and regional resources

| Atmosphere | ↔ | Oceans and seas living marine resources | ↔ | Global and regional resources |

Cross-sectoral linkages

Accelerating sustainable development: International trade; adequate net financial flows; domestic policies (ch. 1.1)

Integration of environment and development in decision-making: Policy, planning and management level; economic instruments and marketing incentives; environmental accounting; legal and regulatory frameworks (ch. 1.2)

Changing consumption patterns: Less wasteful lifestyles; sustainable consumption levels (ch. 2.2)

Demographic dynamics and sustainability: Global challenges; national and local level integration of population and environment (ch. 2.3)

Health: Pollution health risks; communicable diseases; vulnerable groups (ch. 2.4)

Human settlements: Shelter; environmental infrastructure; energy and transport; disaster-prone areas (ch. 3.1)

Urban water supplies: Drinking water; sanitation (ch. 3.2)

Solid waste management: Waste minimization; safe disposal; recycling (ch. 3.3)

Urban pollution and health: Air pollution (ch. 3.4)

Sustainable agriculture and rural development: Land use; conservation and rehabilitation; freshwater; plant and animal genetic resources; pest management; rural energy (ch. 4.3)

Combating deforestation: Multiple utilization of trees, forests and lands; assessment and monitoring; international and regional cooperation (ch. 4.4)

Managing fragile ecosystems (ch. 4.5):

Combating desertification and drought

Information and monitoring; anti-desertification programmes and action plans; drought preparedness and relief (ch. 4.5.1)

Sustainable mountain development

Information; integrated watershed development (ch. 4.5.2)

Biological diversity: Information; conservation (ch. 4.6)

Environmentally sound management of biotechnology: Productivity of food and feed; health; environment protection (ch. 4.7)

Toxic chemicals: Chemical risks assessment; information; risks management programmes (ch. 6.1)

Hazardous wastes: Cleaner production, waste minimization; international cooperation for transboundary movement (ch. 6.2)

Radioactive wastes: International agreements for safe management (ch. 6.3)

Education, public awareness and training (ch. 7.1)

Strengthening the role of major groups: Women; youth; indigenous people and their communities; NGOs; farmers; local authorities; trade unions; business and industry; scientific and technological community (ch. 7.2)

human lifestyles and welfare everywhere. The global dimension and threats of ozone depletion, climate change, transboundary air pollution, marine pollution and depletion of marine living resources requires a responsible commitment and partnership between all nations to curtail harmful activities and to ensure equitable and sustainable utilization of these shared resources.

5.1 PROTECTION OF THE ATMOSPHERE

The shielding atmosphere of our planet is beset today by three interrelated problems: an increase in atmospheric concentrations of the gases that produce greenhouse warming, presaging abnormal and drastic alterations in the Earth's climate; the combustion of fuels, causing extensive local and transboundary air pollution; and emissions of halocarbons that are gradually destroying the stratospheric ozone.

Protection of the atmosphere is a wide, multidimensional endeavour involving many areas of economic activity. It should combine with social and economic development and take full account of the needs of developing countries to achieve sustained economic growth and poverty eradication.

There exists a substantial corpus of environmental and developmental knowledge of the atmosphere. Nevertheless, concern about climate change, air pollution and ozone depletion has created new demands for information. *Addressing the uncertainties: improving the scientific basis for decision-making* is, therefore, a priority. This can be achieved by intensifying scientific and technological research, particularly of the social and economic consequences of changes in the atmosphere. Addressing these problems requires expanded and strengthened research to better understand climate's physical, chemical and biological properties and how they affect ecosystems and human health. It also needs comprehensive observing systems to detect the current state, as well as trends, in the atmosphere and in ecosystems, and further urgent research on the effects of these changes and potential responses.

The greenhouse gases are carbon dioxide, methane, nitrous oxide, halons and atmospheric water vapour. All except halons are naturally occurring. Human activities, however, have changed the net emission rates of these gases to the point where their convergence in the atmosphere is beginning to have serious repercussions on forests, biodiversity, freshwater and marine ecosystems and on economic activities such as agriculture. It is also important to develop new sinks for carbon dioxide and improve existing ones by promoting appropriate terrestrial and marine resource development and land use by increasing forest and soil management activities. Scaling down the rates of deforestation may be a first step, followed by an increase in afforestation programmes. Using fuel wood to replace fossil fuels is another way to reduce carbon dioxide emissions. Other techniques, such as increasing the carbon content of soils, can provide temporary carbon sinks. Countries whose agricultural practices produce high methane emissions should adopt cropping and fertilizing systems to reduce them.

To tackle these problems in a comprehensive and equitable manner, the international community endorsed a legally binding treaty, the United Nations Framework Convention on Climate Change, in Rio de Janeiro in June of 1992. Signed by 153 Member States of the United Nations, as well as the European Economic Community, the Convention aims to stabilize greenhouse gas concentrations in the atmosphere at a level that would prevent dangerous anthropogenic interference with the climate system. The Convention also seeks to achieve this level in a frame of time sufficient to allow ecosystems to adapt naturally to climate change, to ensure that food production is not threatened and to enable economic development to proceed in a sustainable manner.

Efforts to protect the atmosphere can also be enhanced by using materials and resources efficiently in all industries; improving technologies for pollution abatement; replacing chlorofluorocarbons (CFCs) and other ozone-depleting substances with appropriate substitutes, consistent with the 1987 Montreal Protocol; and scaling down industrial by-products and waste. Compliance with control measures within the Montreal Protocol and its 1990 amendments will assist in *preventing stratospheric ozone depletion*. The total chlorine loading of the Earth's atmosphere of ozone-depleting substances, such as CFCs and halons, has continued to rise, with a corresponding increase in ultraviolet radiation reaching the Earth's surface. This has far-reaching consequences on human health—in the marked rise in skin cancers and eye diseases—on agriculture and on micro-organisms living in the surface layers of the ocean, which may in turn affect the entire oceanic food chain.

Transboundary atmospheric pollution harms human health and destroys the environment, causing tree and forest loss and acidifying water bodies. Programmes should strengthen regional agreements for transboundary air pollution control, cooperate with developing countries for systematic observation and assessment and create and exchange emission control technologies for mobile and stationary sources of air pollution. Greater emphasis should be put on addressing the extent, causes, health and socio-economic effects of solar ultraviolet radiation and the acidification of the environment.

Much of the world's energy is currently produced and consumed in ways that are unsustainable. The need to control atmospheric emissions of greenhouse and other gases and substances will be based, increasingly, on efficiency in energy production and use as well as on a growing reliance on environmentally sound and safe energy systems and technologies. Energy sources for *promoting sustainable development* will need to be applied in ways that respect the atmosphere, human health and the environment as a whole.

Transportation, although crucial for any modern economy, is also a source of harmful atmospheric emissions. Traffic and transport systems need to be designed and managed more effectively. Shifting transport to more efficient and less polluting modes, such as rural and urban mass transit systems and environmentally sound road networks, needs to be encouraged. These technical solutions, however, address a minor dimension of the transportation issue. Fundamentally, urban-suburban-industrial development, including the location of dwellings and the workplace, must take not only political and socio-economic considerations into account, but environmental ones as well, such as pollution of the atmosphere, noise and congestion. In order to encourage such broad strategies for growth, it has been proposed that regional conferences be held on transport and the environment.

Countries, in cooperation with the relevant United Nations bodies, international donors and non-governmental organizations, should mobilize technical and financial resources and facilitate technical cooperation with developing countries to reinforce their technical, managerial, planning and administrative capacities and promote sustainable development and the protection of the atmosphere in all relevant sectors.

5.2 PROTECTION OF THE OCEANS AND ALL KINDS OF SEAS, INCLUDING ENCLOSED AND SEMI-ENCLOSED SEAS

The programmes subsumed within the chapter on the protection of the oceans and all kinds of seas represent, collectively, an integrated strategy for the sound management of oceans, and regional and enclosed seas.

The marine environment—the world's oceans, all seas and adjacent coastal areas—comprises an essential component of the global life-support system. The oceans and all seas cover 70 per cent of the planet's surface and play a dominant and decisive role in the Earth's local, regional and global biogeochemical processes. Global energy, climate and weather, the hydrological and carbon cycles, and atmospheric and physical processes are all critically influenced by oceanic processes. Yet our understanding of these processes is less developed than our understanding of those occurring in the terrestrial environment and atmosphere. The long-term management and sustainable development of the world's resources should be based both on a sound understanding of how the ocean shapes global conditions and on a proper evaluation of the potential benefits of marine resources.

Degradation of the marine environment results from a wide range of activities on land, often due to the lack, or the excess, of economic and industrial growth. Human populations and their land use, agriculture, forestry, fisheries, urban development, tourism and industry all influence the marine environment. Of the land-based sources of marine pollution, some 30 per cent arrives through rivers and industrial and urban run-offs; another 20 per cent comes through the atmosphere; and the rest through municipal wastes. Contaminants which pose the greatest threat to the marine environment include sewage, agricultural run-offs, pesticides and fertilizers, synthetic organic compounds, sediment, litter and plastics, metals, radionuclides, oil/hydrocarbons and polycyclic aromatic hydrocarbons. Whereas at an earlier point in history the oceans were regarded as infinitely vast and unlimited in their resources, such as fish, or in their capacity to absorb and recycle waste, current trends in marine pollution have shown that this is no longer the case.

Marine pollution is also caused by shipping and sea-based activities. Approximately 600,000 tons of oil enter the oceans each year as a result of normal shipping operations, accidents and illegal discharges. With regard to offshore oil and gas, the machinery space discharges are currently being regulated internationally. There are also six regional conventions under consideration for the control of platform discharges. The nature and extent of environmental impacts from offshore oil exploration and production generally account for a very small proportion of marine pollution.

Scientific uncertainty—as in the case of climate change and its consequent sea-level rise—has thwarted effective management, and limited the capacity to make useful predictions and assessments of oceanic environmental change. A marginal rise in the level of the sea has the potential to devastate small islands and low-lying coastal areas. Providing the necessary data for global climate models and reducing uncertainty demands a long-term cooperative research commitment based on the differentiated responsibilities of each country.

Marine issues have been a leading sector for international law and serve as a model for sustainable resources management. Ocean management policy must be integrated horizontally, across disciplines, departments and specialized agencies and between the public and private sector, as well as vertically, through national, regional and global levels of governance, all in one coherent system. International law, as reflected in the United Nations Convention on the Law of the Sea, offers the most appropriate and comprehensive framework and legal instrument to effectively integrate the protection of the environment from pollution, whether land-based, oceanic or atmospheric, with economic development of living and non-living ocean resources. The Convention establishes an important balance between the rights of States and their obligations, including those relating to conservation of the marine environment and its resources. Its implementation at national, regional and international levels requires new strategies that are integrated in content, and precautionary and anticipatory in ambit, for marine and coastal area management and development.

To protect the marine environment requires an anticipatory rather than a reactive approach, and should involve the adoption of precautionary measures, environmental impact assessments, quality criteria for classified substances and a comprehensive approach to address the damaging impacts of air, land and water. Systematic data on marine environmental parameters will be needed to apply integrated management approaches and predict the effects of global climate change on fisheries. In order to determine the role of the oceans in driving global systems and to predict natural and man-induced changes in marine and coastal ecosystems, mechanisms that collect, synthesize and disseminate ocean information from research and monitoring activities need to be restructured and reinforced considerably.

A coordinated institutional approach, integrating all relevant environmental and developmental aspects of ocean and sea resources, is essential. There is a need to improve international coordination among the institutions dealing with oceans and coastal areas; for reinforcing the links between international institutions and Governments; and ensuring that all levels operate in an integrated and multi-disciplinary way.

Marine environmental protection, against the adverse effects of human land-based and sea-based activities, is the first priority in preserving development options, conserving marine ecosystems and safeguarding human health while providing for the rational use of living and non-living marine resources. Governments should monitor, take inventories, and assess the hazards of sea- and land-based marine pollution sources and regularly update national, regional and global assessments of the state of the marine environment. They should establish regulatory and monitoring programmes and treatment facilities to reduce and control effluents, toxic and bio-accumulatory pesticides and fertilizers, chemicals such as synthetic organic compounds, sewage and solid wastes, air pollutants, oil and other hazardous substances. Governments should also update, strengthen and extend the Montreal guidelines and initiate and promote regional and national programmes of actions such as the Regional Seas Programme. As concerns dumping, States should support wider ratification, implementation and participation in relevant Conventions, including the early conclusion of a future strategy for the London Dumping Convention. A global network of contingency plans and response centres for marine pollution accidents should be established, as well as an international regulatory framework for offshore activities.

A second priority is *addressing critical uncertainties for the management of the marine environment and climate change*. This involves the coordination of national and regional scientific programmes to research and observe coastal and near-term phenomena related to climate change, as well as to examine the research parameters essential for ocean and coastal management, both within and beyond the limits of national jurisdiction. Governments should exchange the data and information resulting from national scientific research and monitoring, as well as from traditional ecological knowledge at all levels of management. They should also provide improved forecasts of marine conditions to enhance the safety of the inhabitants of coastal areas and improve the efficiency of maritime operations.

A third priority is *strengthening international, including regional, cooperation and coordination* and relates to the creation of improved mechanisms for strategic planning, and the identification of priorities for legal and institutional initiatives relating to different sectors of marine and coastal activity. Major future developments are likely to occur at the regional level particularly in relation to land-based and atmospheric pollution of the marine environment and fisheries management.

Governments should promote the effective exchange of information and, where appropriate, the building of institutional linkages between regional institutions concerned with environment and development in marine and coastal areas. They should ensure the effective operation of coordinating mechanisms and reporting arrangements for the components of the United Nations system dealing with environment and development in marine and coastal areas, and enhance their links with other concerned organizations, including donor and assistance agencies. General marine and coastal issues, including their environmental and developmental aspects, should enjoy regular consideration within the United Nations system at the intergovernmental level. Governments should also strengthen existing intergovernmental regional cooperation and coordination among all relevant organizations and bodies, development assistance and donor agencies, and the private sector. National Governments, when necessary, should be assisted in implementing the principles of relevant international agreements, as reflected in the United Nations Convention on the Law of the Sea. Centres of excellence on marine science and technology should also be established.

5.3 PROTECTION, RATIONAL USE AND DEVELOPMENT OF LIVING MARINE RESOURCES

There is a wide spectrum of different types of life forms in the oceans. About 20,000 species of freshwater and saltwater living resources have been identified while many more species remain to be discovered. Of the roughly 9,000 species that are harvested, only 22 support significant fisheries. The commercial harvest of fishes, crustaceans and molluscs in 1990 amounted to 98 million metric tons, which is equivalent to the estimated sustainable annual yield from conventional fisheries. Over 80 per cent of the commercial harvest is marine catch, mainly from the coastal and shelf seas within the Exclusive Economic Zones (EEZs) as outlined in the Law of the Sea Convention. The high-seas fisheries represent only about 5 per cent of the total world landings.

Mariculture today yields approximately 5 million metric tons per year and is expected to double by the end of this century. In addition, artisanal fisheries yield approximately 24 million metric tons annually and are socially the most important since they contribute significantly to fisheries employment and are critical to balanced food nutrition, particularly in coastal developing countries.

The rise in marine catches over the last two decades has largely been the result of discoveries of new resources, the introduction of new fishing technologies, and the implementation of the Law of the Sea Convention. Nevertheless, the management of high-seas fisheries, including the adoption, monitoring and enforcement of effective conservation measures remains insufficient in many areas, and some resources are overused. In addition, there are inadequacies in fishing practices, biological knowledge, fisheries statistics and systems for handling data.

The above problems extend beyond fisheries. Coral reefs and other coastal habitats such as mangroves and estuaries are among the most highly diverse, integrated and productive of the Earth's ecosystems. They often serve important ecological functions, provide coastal protection, and are critical resources for food, energy, tourism and economic development. In various parts of the world, such coastal systems are increasingly under duress. Estuarine and near-shore environments and enclosed and semi-enclosed seas have been particularly degraded.

Many countries face mounting problems related to their rights and obligations, including local overfishing, poor management performance, unauthorized incursions by foreign vessels, ecosystem degradation, increased stock fluctuations, over-capitalization, excessive fleet sizes, insufficiently selective gear, inadequate resource information and increasing competition between artisanal and industrial fishing and between fishing and other types of activities.

At present, fisheries account for some 16 per cent of the total animal protein consumption in the world. This contribution is about the same as for beef and pork. The diversity of fish species is important, in that it provides consumers with a wider choice in taste preference. About a quarter of the world's marine production is processed into meal for livestock.

The sustainable use and conservation of marine living resources of the high seas is of social, economic and nutritional importance: marine living resources can make a significant contribution to national food security. The use of marine species for human food should be increased by promoting direct consumption, avoiding wastage and improving techniques of harvest, handling and transportation. As the world's population rises to some 6.3 billion by 2000, it will become increasingly necessary to maximize food production from all sources, especially in light of existing pressures on agricultural land resources.

Emphasis should be on multi-species management and other approaches that take into account the relationships among species. These issues are important to preserve the biological diversity and ecological integrity of coastal and marine ecosystems by protecting critical habitats and endangered species.

With regard to high-seas living marine resources, States should promote their sustainable use and conservation. To this end, they should develop and increase the potential of marine living resources to meet human nutritional needs as well as social, economic and development goals. They should also maintain or restore populations of marine species at levels which can produce the maximum sustainable yield as qualified by relevant environmental and economic factors, taking into consideration relationships among species. They should also promote the development and use of selective fishing gear and practices that minimize waste in the catch of target species and minimize the by-catch of non-target species, ensure effective monitoring and enforcement with respect to fishing activities and protect and restore endangered marine species, preserve habitats and other ecologically sensitive areas and promote scientific research.

States whose nationals and vessels fish on the high seas should give full effect to the provisions of the Law of the Sea Convention with regard to issues relating to marine resources on the high seas, in particular the straddling fish stocks—or the fisheries population whose ranges lie both within and beyond exclusive economic zones—and highly migratory species. Action, as well as cooperation, by States at the bilateral, sub-regional, regional and global levels is also essential to resolve these issues.

With regard to the *sustainable use and conservation of marine living resources under national jurisdiction*, States should ensure that developing countries and States whose economies are overwhelmingly dependent on the exploitation of marine living resources of their EEZs should obtain the full social and economic benefits through sustainable use of coastal marine resources, exclusive economic zones and other areas under national jurisdiction.

In ensuring the conservation and sustainable use of these resources, States should accomplish similar goals as stated above for high-seas living marine resources. In addition they should take into account traditional knowledge and interests of local communities, small-scale artisanal fisheries and indigenous people in development and management programmes and enhance the productivity and utilization of their marine living resources for food and income. The use of marine resources for pharmaceutical, tourism and recreation should not be overlooked but rather enhanced. Throughout these programmes, care should be taken to integrate the protection and sustainable management of coral reefs and other critical ecosystems into living resources and coastal zone management strategies.

Human resources should be targeted at developing and managing marine living resources, training entrepreneurs, upgrading managers and environmental issues and developing a core of scientists to assess marine living resources. Coastal development planning should fully involve fishermen, women, indigenous people and local communities, recognizing their important rights and responsibilities. It should include small-scale fisheries training and extension services and aquaculture development.

6

MANAGING CHEMICALS AND WASTES

THE use of chemicals is essential in the development process and in the promotion of human well-being. They are extensively used by all societies, irrespective of their stage of development. However, toxic materials and by-products, if improperly handled, can have adverse effects on human health and harmful consequences for the environment. Hazardous chemical waste can contaminate soil and groundwater and find its way to the bottom sediments of rivers and lakes. Released as sewage, it can poison or kill valuable living marine resources, either directly or by moving through the food chain. Radioactive waste can also be highly toxic, and requires extremely careful handling and disposal. Over the years, the growing prevalence of these materials in industrial societies has not been matched by effective policies to dispose of them appropriately, and has resulted occasionally in some severe accidents.

It is vitally important to cut back on the production of dangerous industrial wastes and improve their safe and proper handling and disposal if human health and the environment are to be protected. The safe handling and management of toxic, hazardous and radioactive wastes is critical at all stages, from production, transport, recycling, treatment and storage to

Managing chemicals and wastes

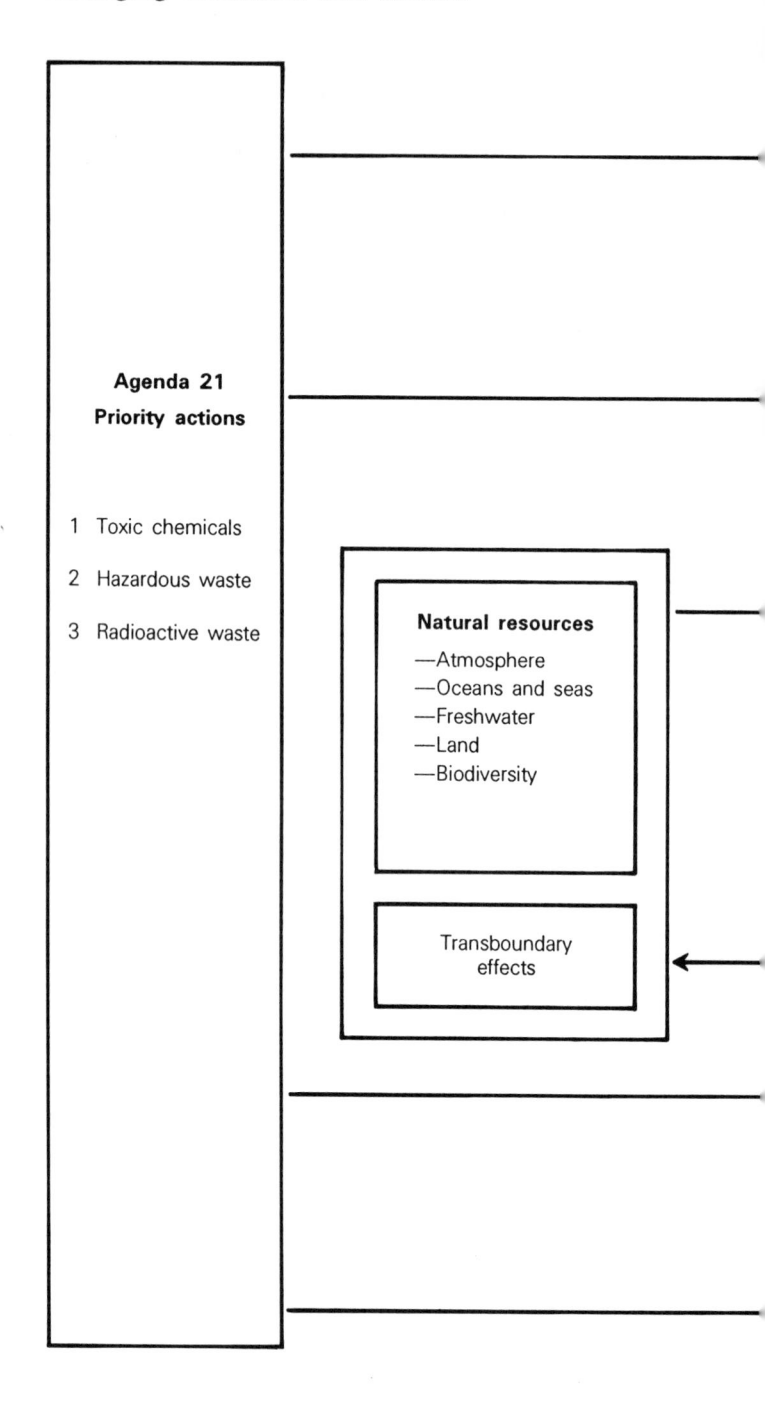

**Agenda 21
Priority actions**

1 Toxic chemicals
2 Hazardous waste
3 Radioactive waste

Natural resources
—Atmosphere
—Oceans and seas
—Freshwater
—Land
—Biodiversity

Transboundary effects

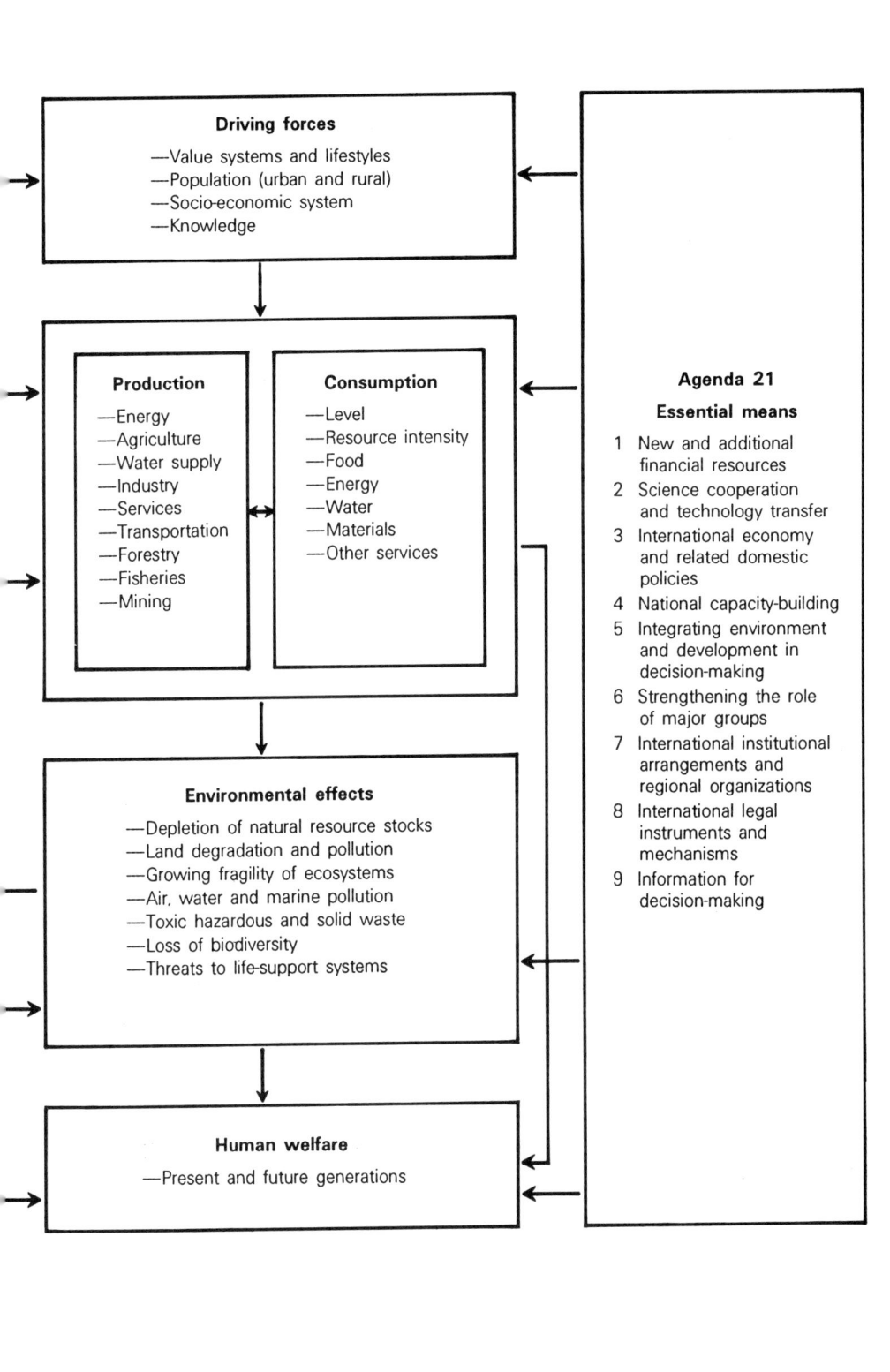

Driving forces
—Value systems and lifestyles
—Population (urban and rural)
—Socio-economic system
—Knowledge

Production
—Energy
—Agriculture
—Water supply
—Industry
—Services
—Transportation
—Forestry
—Fisheries
—Mining

Consumption
—Level
—Resource intensity
—Food
—Energy
—Water
—Materials
—Other services

Environmental effects
—Depletion of natural resource stocks
—Land degradation and pollution
—Growing fragility of ecosystems
—Air, water and marine pollution
—Toxic hazardous and solid waste
—Loss of biodiversity
—Threats to life-support systems

Human welfare
—Present and future generations

Agenda 21
Essential means

1. New and additional financial resources
2. Science cooperation and technology transfer
3. International economy and related domestic policies
4. National capacity-building
5. Integrating environment and development in decision-making
6. Strengthening the role of major groups
7. International institutional arrangements and regional organizations
8. International legal instruments and mechanisms
9. Information for decision-making

Managing chemicals and wastes

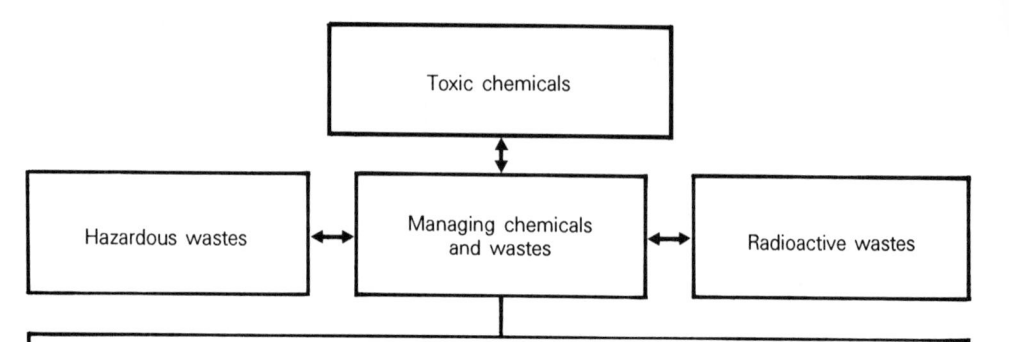

```
                    ┌─────────────────┐
                    │ Toxic chemicals │
                    └────────┬────────┘
                             ↕
┌──────────────────┐  ┌──────────────────┐  ┌──────────────────┐
│ Hazardous wastes │↔ │ Managing chemicals│↔ │ Radioactive wastes│
│                  │  │   and wastes     │  │                  │
└──────────────────┘  └────────┬─────────┘  └──────────────────┘
                               │
```

Cross-sectoral linkages

Accelerating sustainable development: International trade; adequate net financial flows; domestic policies (ch. 1.1)

Integration of environment and development in decision-making: Policy, planning and management level; economic instruments and marketing incentives; environmental accounting; legal and regulatory frameworks (ch. 1.2)

Changing consumption patterns: Less wasteful lifestyles; sustainable consumption levels (ch. 2.2)

Health: Pollution health risks (ch. 2.4)

Human settlements: Disaster-prone areas (ch. 3.1)

Urban water supplies: Drinking water (ch. 3.2)

Solid waste management: Waste minimization; safe disposal; expansion of services; recycling (ch. 3.3)

Urban pollution and health: Air pollution; municipal health planning; radiation protection (ch. 3.4)

Freshwater resources: Protection of quality and resources (ch. 4.2)

Environmentally sound management of biotechnology: Productivity of food and feed; health; environment protection; safety; enabling mechanisms; international cooperation (ch. 4.7)

Atmosphere: Industry; ozone depletion; addressing uncertainties (ch. 5.1)

Oceans and seas: Marine protection; living resources; uncertainties and climate change (ch. 5.2)

Education, public awareness and training (ch. 7.1)

Strengthening the role of major groups: Women; youth; indigenous people and their communities; NGOs; farmers; local authorities; trade unions; business and industry; scientific and technological community (ch. 7.2)

final disposal. Collaborative action is required by Governments, private industry and international organizations. It is essential to assess the dangers of hundreds of chemicals, strengthen the exchange of information about these dangers internationally, establish a consistent system of labelling substances and promote safer alternatives to harmful chemical use.

Minimizing the danger posed by the world's growing volume of radioactive waste requires ever greater vigilance in enforcing international safety standards. To protect human health and the environment, the safe management and disposal of radioactive waste should be an integral part of world-wide nuclear safety efforts. By 1995, some 481 billion cubic metres of low- and intermediate-level radioactive waste will be generated annually. About two thirds will be produced in the industrialized countries of western Europe and Japan, and one third in eastern Europe and the developing countries. The main sources are nuclear power generation, medical centres, research institutions, mines and industrial facilities.

Scaling down pollution and waste will require a transition to environmentally sound technologies in all areas of human activity, including industry, agriculture, energy, and transportation. In a number of cases, the cumulative effect of past malpractice and pollution has underscored the urgency for actions to avoid the permanent degradation and destruction of the environment. The industrialized countries with their experience and wide range of new and innovative waste minimization technologies and policies must forge partnerships to ensure that growth in developing countries does not follow this pollution-generating path.

6.1 ENVIRONMENTALLY SOUND MANAGEMENT OF TOXIC CHEMICALS, INCLUDING PREVENTION OF ILLEGAL INTERNATIONAL TRAFFIC IN TOXIC AND DANGEROUS PRODUCTS

The environmentally sound management of toxic chemicals is essential to undo the mistakes of the past and harness chemicals for use in sustainable development. Of the several thousand naturally occurring or commercial chemical substances, many are hazardous and have polluted and contaminated food, commercial products and the environment.

Human exposure to these toxic chemicals has, fortunately, been limited, since most are used in very small amounts. Over 95 per cent of the world's chemical production involves the use of some 1500 chemicals. However, the lack of crucial data for risk assessment of many high-volume production chemicals poses a serious problem. This situation is further exacerbated by the deficiency of resources to assess chemicals for which data is available.

The introduction of chemicals and of chemically related industries in developing countries that lack sufficient infrastructure and trained human resources for chemical safety is also of some concern. Gross chemical contaminations, gravely damaging human health, genetic structures and reproductive capacity as well as the overall environment, have occurred in recent years in a number of countries.

Effective chemicals control and risk management urgently require increased international collaboration and the improvement of national capacities and capabilities. A prerequisite for the environmentally sound management of toxic chemicals is the reliable assessment of health and environmental risk. International activities need to be strengthened to adequately support programmes for the risk assessment of chemicals in Member States throughout the world.

A coordinated approach should be adopted to reinforce information exchange, harmonize labelling systems, prioritize efforts for risk reduction, strengthen industry's responsible care and product stewardship and intensify education, training and public awareness. Harmonizing control procedures in trade, preventing accidents and honing emergency response procedures are also important. There is a need for national and local emergency response capabilities to resolve and counteract the impact of chemical accidents. Training courses and direct public information campaigns are important in this regard to build up an awareness of the problems of chemical safety, including the provision of information on chemical stockpiles and environmentally safe alternatives and emission inventories.

The preceding issues are all closely linked. To successfully implement them will require intensive international collaboration, better coordination of current international activities, and further identification and application—in particular among developing countries—of appropriate technical, scientific, educational and financial means.

Governments, in concert with relevant international organizations and industry, should work at *expanding and accelerating international assessment of chemical risks* by strengthening and expanding programmes on chemical risk assessment within the United Nations system, together with other international organizations, as well as promoting mechanisms to increase collaboration among Governments, industry, academia and relevant non-governmental organizations. By 2000, several hundred priority chemicals or groups of chemicals should be assessed, including major pollutants and contaminants of global significance. Guidelines should be prepared for an acceptable exposure for a greater number of chemical substances, based on a peer review and scientific consensus, and should distinguish between health and environment-based exposure limits and those related to socio-economic factors.

Safe chemical use mandates the *harmonization of classification and labelling of chemicals*. Adequate labelling of chemicals, based on assessed hazards to health and the environment, is the simplest and most efficient way of indicating how to handle and use them safely. International organizations, with active participation of Governments and non-governmental organizations, should work to establish and elaborate a harmonized classification and compatible labelling system for chemicals. The new system should draw on current systems, be developed and implemented in steps and aim to be compatible with existing labels.

Governments, in cooperation with international organizations, should promote the *information exchange on toxic chemicals and chemical risks*, covering the scientific, technical, economic and legal dimensions. With the aim of fully implementing the Prior Informed Consent procedure—contained in the amended London Guidelines for the Exchange of Information on Chemicals in International Trade, and in the Food and Agriculture Organization's International Code of Conduct on the Distribution and Use of Pesticides—Governments, industries and international organizations should strengthen national and international institutions and networks responsible for information exchange on toxic chemicals, and cooperate technically with, and provide information to, other countries.

To reduce unacceptable or unreasonable chemical risk as much as is economically possible, Governments should work at the *establishment of risk reduction programmes* that employ a broad-based approach, involve a wide range of risk reduction options and take precautionary measures derived from broad-based life-cycle analyses. Governments should work to replace toxic chemicals with less hazardous substitutes, adopt policies that are based on precautionary and anticipatory principles, develop emergency response procedures and adopt regulatory frameworks for the prevention of accidents. International organizations should coordinate concerted risk reduction activities, including the development of policies for manufacturers, importers and other users of toxic chemicals.

All countries should aim at the *strengthening of national capabilities and capacities for the management of chemicals*, by the year 2000, by introducing national systems for the environmentally sound management of chemicals, including legislation and provisions for implementation and enforcement. Governments, together with intergovernmental organizations, agencies and programmes of the United Nations, should work to develop, strengthen and promote the basic elements for a nationally sound management of chemicals. These elements include adequate legislation, information gathering and dissemination, risk assessment and interpretation capacity, risk management policies, implementation and enforcement capability and the capacity to rehabilitate contaminated sites and affected populations.

According to their capacities and available resources, and with the cooperation of the United Nations and other relevant organizations, Governments should reinforce national capacities for the *prevention of illegal international traffic in toxic and dangerous products* that are detrimental to public health and the environment, particularly in developing countries. This implies strengthening national capacities to detect and halt any illegal attempt to introduce toxic and dangerous products into the territory of any country, in contravention of national legislation and relevant international legal instruments, and assisting all countries, particularly developing countries, in obtaining all appropriate information concerning illegal traffic in toxic and dangerous products.

6.2 ENVIRONMENTALLY SOUND MANAGEMENT OF HAZARDOUS WASTES, INCLUDING PREVENTION OF ILLEGAL INTERNATIONAL TRAFFIC IN HAZARDOUS WASTES

The environmentally sound management of hazardous wastes is of paramount importance for proper health, environmental protection, natural resource management and sustainable development. Hazardous wastes are often indiscriminately dumped into rivers, abandoned along roadsides and poured directly into oceans. They threaten the health and safety of all people. Millions of tons of potentially hazardous wastes cross national borders each year on their way to be recycled or disposed. Many countries, despite promulgating laws, lack the ability to enforce legal provisions, have little or no record of how much or what types of wastes are being produced and do not possess adequate facilities to manage wastes in an environmentally sound manner. The problem of hazardous waste management involves not only the waste generated today but also the legacy of wastes inappropriately disposed of in the past.

The integrity of the environment and human health are threatened by the increasing amount of hazardous wastes produced and improperly managed. This is to a large extent due to the lack of national capacity to handle and manage hazardous wastes. It includes inadequate infrastructure, deficiencies in regulatory frameworks, insufficient training and education programmes and lack of coordination. In addition, there is a scarcity of information on environmental contamination and pollution and associated health risks from exposure. The lack of harmonization of existing criteria for monitoring capabilities and identifying hazardous wastes hampers efforts to prevent their illegal transboundary movement.

An international strategy should be developed for the environmentally sound management of hazardous wastes. This involves four priority areas. The first aims at *promoting the prevention and minimization of hazardous waste* as part of a broader approach to change industrial processes and consumer patterns, such as pollution prevention and cleaner production technologies. Processing wastes into useful recycled material should feature prominently in this strategy. The "cleaner production" concept includes a "cradle-to-grave" approach for minimizing emissions into the air, water and soil, as well as for reducing energy consumption and use of raw materials.

Hazardous waste minimization, reuse, recycling and the use of cleaner production methods all have important economic consequences in terms of costs and benefits. The economic benefits of environmentally sound management of hazardous wastes relate primarily to the reduction of both health hazards, acute and chronic, and adverse effects on natural resources, such as arable land and wildlife. The economic costs relate to the processing of wastes and the adoption of appropriate production technologies. There is a need to enhance knowledge and information on the economics of prevention and the management of hazardous wastes. The adoption of requisite production technologies by developing countries should not deter their industrial development. This will require technical cooperation and multilateral financial assistance.

The second priority aims at *promoting and strengthening institutional capacities in hazardous waste management*. Governments should work to adopt appropriate coordinating, legislative and regulatory measures and introduce public awareness campaigns and information programmes at the national level.

The third priority is *promoting and strengthening international cooperation in the management of transboundary movements of hazardous wastes*. This requires harmonizing criteria for the identification of hazardous wastes which are dangerous to the environment, building monitoring capacities and developing international legal instruments. Governments should adopt policies to effect a ban, or prohibition, on the export of hazardous wastes to countries that do not have the capacity to deal with these wastes in an environmentally sound way, or that have altogether banned the import of such wastes.

Existing agreements on hazardous wastes, such as the Basel and Bamako Conventions, should receive early ratification, and Governments should pursue the expeditious elaboration of related mechanisms, guidelines and protocols, including the Protocol on liability and compensation, to facilitate the implementation of these agreements.

The fourth priority area for an international strategy for the environmentally sound management of hazardous wastes is *preventing illegal international traffic in hazardous wastes*, which may cause serious threats to human health and the environment and impose an abnormal burden on countries receiving such shipments. National capacities should be strengthened to detect and halt any illegal attempt to introduce hazardous wastes into any country, in contravention of national legislation and relevant international legal instruments. Countries that suffer the consequences of illegal traffic, particularly developing countries, should be assisted, within the framework of the Basel Convention.

6.3 SAFE AND ENVIRONMENTALLY SOUND MANAGEMENT OF RADIOACTIVE WASTES

Radioactive wastes are generated in the nuclear fuel cycle as well as in nuclear applications (the use of radionuclides in medicine, research and industry). The radiological and safety risks from radioactive wastes vary from very low in short-lived, low-level wastes up to very large for high-level wastes. Annually about 200,000 m³ of low-level and intermediate-level waste and 10,000 m³ of high-level waste (as well as spent nuclear fuel destined for final disposal) is generated worldwide from nuclear power production. These volumes are increasing as more nuclear power units are taken into operation, nuclear facilities are decommissioned and the use of radionuclides increases. High-level waste contains about 99 per cent radionuclides and thus presents the largest radiological risk. Waste volumes from nuclear applications are generally much smaller, typically some tens of cubic metres or less per year and country. However, the activity concentration, especially in sealed radiation sources, might be high, thus justifying very stringent radiological protection measures. The growth of waste volumes should continue to be kept under close review.

Promoting the safe and environmentally sound management of radioactive wastes, including their minimization, transportation and disposal, is important given their characteristics. In most countries with a substantive nuclear power programme, technical and administrative measures have been taken to implement a waste management system. In many other countries, with national nuclear programmes still only in preparation or with only nuclear applications, such systems are still needed.

All countries generating radioactive waste should adopt an interactive and integrated approach to the safe management, transportation, storage and disposal of radioactive wastes, within a wider framework for nuclear safety, to protect human health and the environment. The priority activities should promote policies and practical measures to minimize and limit the generation of radioactive wastes and provide for their safe processing, conditioning and disposal. Governments should strengthen their efforts to implement the Code of Practice for International Transboundary Movement of Radioactive Waste. They should also promote research and development of methods for the safe and environmentally sound treatment, processing and disposal, including deep geological disposal, of high-level radioactive waste, and conduct research and assessment programmes concerned with evaluating the health and environmental impacts of radioactive waste disposal.

Developed countries should cooperate with developing countries in establishing or strengthening their radioactive waste management infrastructures, including legislation, organizations, trained manpower and facilities for the handling of wastes generated from nuclear applications.

7

PEOPLE'S PARTICIPATION AND RESPONSIBILITY

HUMAN society is unfathomably rich in diverse social communities and experiences that can help Governments in their quest for environmentally sound and sustainable development. Building environmental and economic security requires a social partnership that makes use of contributions of all peoples and assures that each will share in the benefits. This applies particularly to women, youth, indigenous peoples and their communities, non-governmental organizations, farmers, local authorities, trade unions, business, industry and the scientific and technological community.

To assure the full and equal protection of women in all development activities, their numbers should be augmented in decision-making, technical positions and in the field. National reviews should be held of the legal, educational and cultural barriers—as well as attitudes—faced by women in public life, and of ways to overcome those barriers. At the same time, it is necessary to eliminate female illiteracy, expand the enrolment of women and girls at every level of schooling and revise academic curricula to bar gender stereotypes.

Young people need to participate actively in decisions that will determine their future. They could be actively associated with development planning and resource management at the national, regional and local levels.

People's participation and responsibility

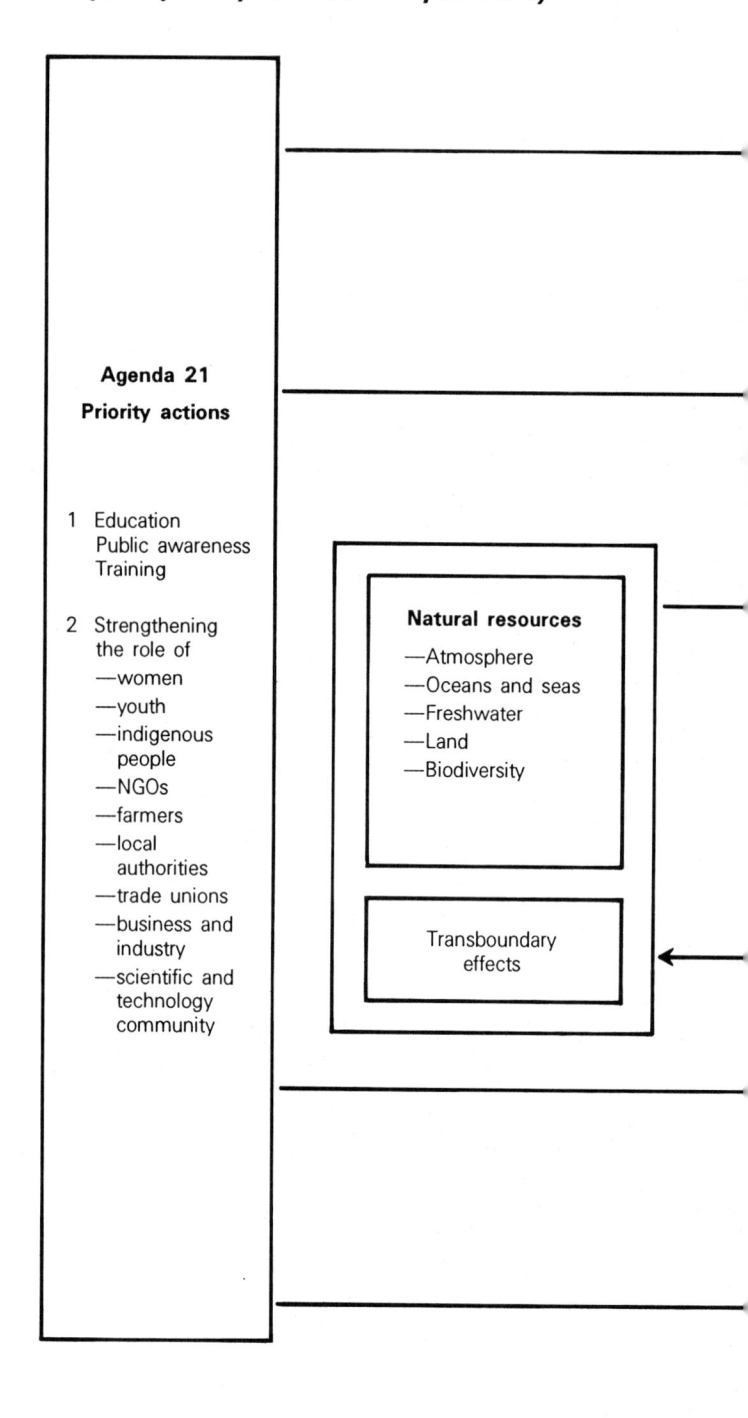

**Agenda 21
Priority actions**

1. Education
   Public awareness
   Training

2. Strengthening
   the role of
   —women
   —youth
   —indigenous
     people
   —NGOs
   —farmers
   —local
     authorities
   —trade unions
   —business and
     industry
   —scientific and
     technology
     community

Natural resources
—Atmosphere
—Oceans and seas
—Freshwater
—Land
—Biodiversity

Transboundary
effects

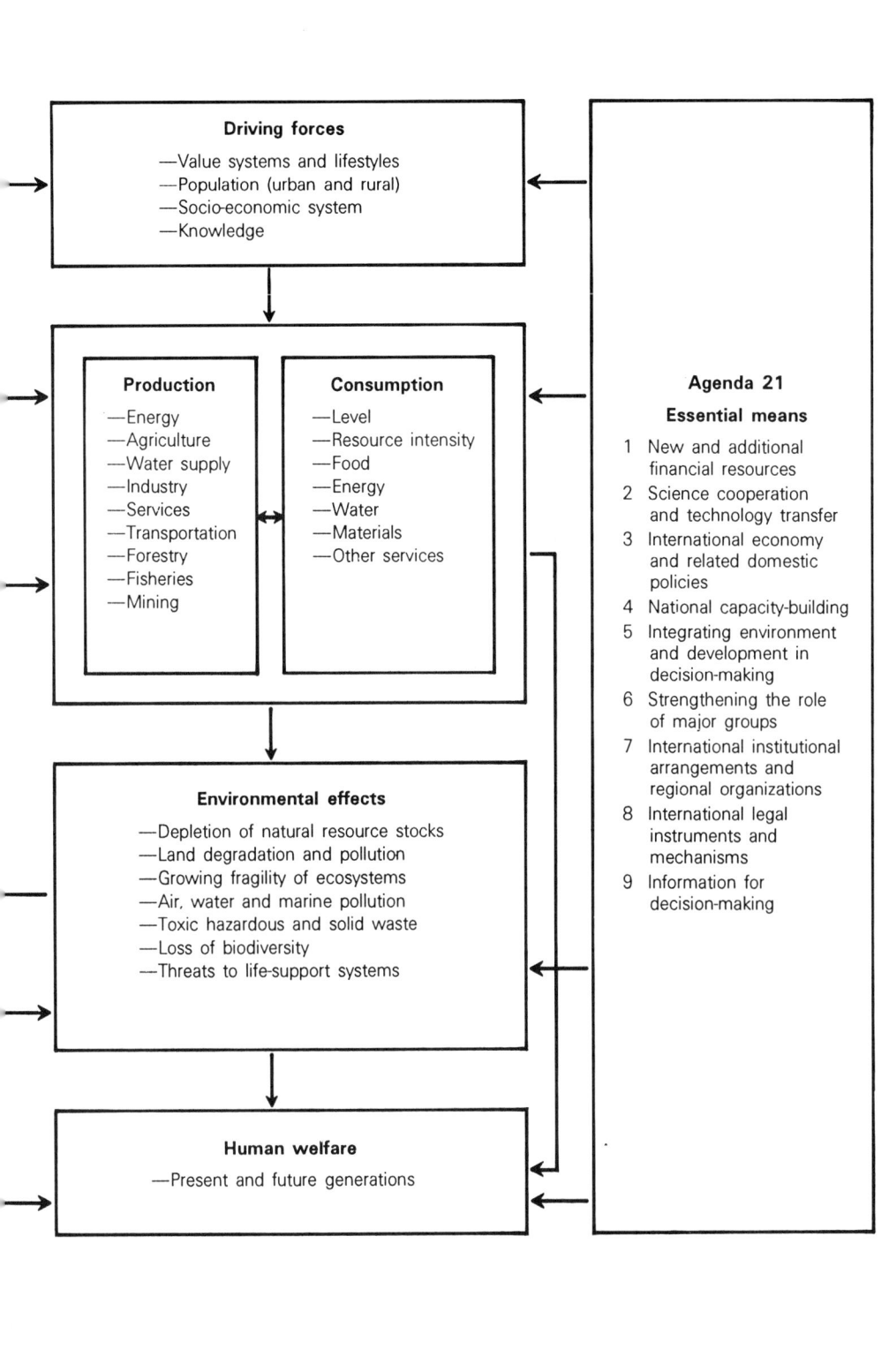

Driving forces
- Value systems and lifestyles
- Population (urban and rural)
- Socio-economic system
- Knowledge

Production
- Energy
- Agriculture
- Water supply
- Industry
- Services
- Transportation
- Forestry
- Fisheries
- Mining

Consumption
- Level
- Resource intensity
- Food
- Energy
- Water
- Materials
- Other services

Environmental effects
- Depletion of natural resource stocks
- Land degradation and pollution
- Growing fragility of ecosystems
- Air, water and marine pollution
- Toxic hazardous and solid waste
- Loss of biodiversity
- Threats to life-support systems

Human welfare
- Present and future generations

Agenda 21
Essential means
1. New and additional financial resources
2. Science cooperation and technology transfer
3. International economy and related domestic policies
4. National capacity-building
5. Integrating environment and development in decision-making
6. Strengthening the role of major groups
7. International institutional arrangements and regional organizations
8. International legal instruments and mechanisms
9. Information for decision-making

People's participation and responsibility

> Strengthening the role
> of major groups:
> women; youth; indigenous people;
> ngos; farmers; local authorities;
> trade unions; business and industry;
> scientific and technological community

> Education
> public awareness
> training

Cross-sectoral linkages

Accelerating sustainable development: International trade; adequate net financial flows; domestic policies (ch. 1.1)

Integration of environment and development in decision-making: Policy, planning and management level; economic instruments and marketing incentives; environmental accounting; legal and regulatory frameworks (ch. 1.2)

Combating poverty: Providing sustainable livelihoods (ch. 2.1)

Changing consumption patterns: Less wasteful lifestyles; sustainable consumption levels; informed consumer choices (ch. 2.2)

Demographic dynamics and sustainability: National and local level integration of population and environment (ch. 2.3)

Health: Pollution health risks; basic needs; communicable diseases; vulnerable groups (ch. 2.4)

Human settlements: Shelter; land and settlement management; environmental infrastructure; energy and transport; human resources and capacity-building; disaster-prone areas (ch. 3.1)

Urban water supplies: Drinking water; sanitation (ch. 3.2)

Solid waste management: Waste minimization; safe disposal; expansion of services; recycling (ch. 3.3)

Urban pollution and health: Air pollution; municipal health planning; radiation protection (ch. 3.4)

Land resources: Integrated planning and management (ch. 4.1)

Freshwater resources: Integrated assessment, development and management; protection of quality and resources; drinking water; sanitation; water for agriculture (ch. 4.2)

Sustainable agriculture and rural development: Policy, planning and programming; human resources participation; plant and animal genetic resources; pest management; plant nutrition; rural energy; rural employment; food security (ch. 4.3)

Combating deforestation: Multiple utilization of trees, forests and lands; assessment and monitoring; international and regional cooperation (ch. 4.4)

Managing fragile ecosystems (ch. 4.5)

Combating desertification and drought

Information and monitoring; afforestation and reforestation; alternative livelihoods; anti-desertification programmes and action plans; drought preparedness and relief (ch. 4.5.1)

Sustainable mountain development

Information; integrated watershed development; alternative livelihoods (ch. 4.5.2)

Biological diversity: Information; benefits and use; conservation; capacity-building (ch. 4.6)

Environmentally sound management of biotechnology: Productivity of food and feed; health; environment protection; safety enabling mechanisms; international cooperation (ch. 4.7)

Atmosphere: Sustainable energy development and consumption; transport systems; industry; agriculture; ozone depletion; addressing uncertainties (ch. 5.1)

Oceans and seas: Coastal area development; marine protection; living resources; uncertainties and climate change; international cooperation and coordination; island development (ch. 5.2)

Toxic chemicals: Chemical risks assessment; classification and labelling; information; risks management programmes (ch. 6.1)

Hazardous wastes: Cleaner production, waste minimization, institutional capacities; international cooperation for transboundary movement (ch. 6.2)

Radioactive wastes: International agreements for safe management (ch. 6.3)

Most indigenous peoples and their communities have a special relationship with the environment in their original and ancestral territories. They should be empowered to participate in formulating and implementing laws and policies on resource management and development; they should also be fully involved in consultation, collaboration and cooperation. Their indigenous rights should be ratified and complied with, and legal instruments should be evolved to protect their traditional and environment-related knowledge.

Local, national and international non-governmental organizations possess a wealth of experience that should be used in all aspects of policy-making, as well as in executing the programmes of Agenda 21.

At the community level, local authorities possess skills and experience crucial in turning policies into actions. Local planning, policies and regulations for resource use should be designed to achieve sustainable development. Environmental awareness should start at the household and community levels.

Trade unions are critical to any reorientation of development policies. They are experienced in dealing with industrial change, in promoting environmental protection, safe workplaces and full employment. To ensure participation of workers, Governments and employers should recognize the rights of their employees to organize unions.

Business and industry have a dynamic role in the economic development of a country. They are also pivotal in protecting the environment and human health. They should, however, encourage the use of cleaner processes and technologies at all stages of production, preserve resources and minimize pollution and waste.

The knowledge and innovations emanating from the international scientific and technological community are inestimable. Ethical principles and guidelines governing science and technology in relation to environment and development and which are universally acceptable are critical to achieving sustainable development.

Farmers are the stewards of much of the land, and through their knowledge they can provide the key to implementing sound agricultural policies. Increasing their influence in decision-making will contribute to sustainable development. Training and economic incentives to encourage the use of low-cost, low-energy farming practices and technologies that increase land productivity in a sustainable way should also be promoted.

Implementing a successful action plan for environmentally sound and sustainable development will require a greater popular participation by all the above sectors of society, in all stages of policy development and implementation. A coordinated, participatory approach to policy development, combined with greater transparency and accountability, would ensure successful and well-considered decision-making.

7.1 PROMOTING EDUCATION, PUBLIC AWARENESS AND TRAINING

Education, public awareness and training should be recognized as a process by which human beings and societies reach their fullest potential. Education is critical for promoting sustainable development and improving the capacity of the people to address environment and development issues. It is also crucial for achieving environmental and ethical awareness, values and attitudes, skills and behaviour consistent with sustainable development and for effective public participation in decision-making.

While recognizing that countries as well as regional and international organizations will develop their own priorities and schedules, it is essential to incorporate sustainable development concepts into all levels of education, from basic to tertiary, and for all groups of society. This requires the development of new and alternative teaching methods and the strengthening of community involvement. The potential for indigenous knowledge to contribute to educational efforts should not be overlooked. In addition, Governments might, where necessary, help relevant non-governmental organizations to promote their access to and involvement in the educational system.

A major priority is *reorienting education towards sustainable development* by improving the capacity of a country to address environment and development in its educational programmes, particularly in basic learning. This is indispensable in enabling people to adapt to a swiftly changing world and developing an ethical awareness consistent with the sustainable use of natural resources. Education should, in all disciplines, deal with the dynamics of both the physical/biological and socio-economic environment and human development, including spiritual development. It should employ both formal and non-formal methods and effective means of communication.

Governments should strive to ensure universal access to basic education and reduce current adult illiteracy rates by at least 50 per cent. They might prepare or update national strategies for environmental and development education, both formal and non-formal, reviewing needs, policies and current activities. Advisory national education coordinating bodies or roundtables, representative of all sectors, should be encouraged to promote partnerships, mobilize resources and provide information and a focal point for international ties. Schools should be assisted in designing environmental activity work plans, with the participation of students and staff, and incorporate them throughout the curriculum. They should employ proven and innovative interactive teaching methods. Governments could support university activities and networks, and establish or strengthen national or regional centres of excellence for interdisciplinary research and education on environment and development issues. The United Nations system should undertake a comprehensive review of its educational activities and establish a programme within two years to integrate the decisions of the Rio Conference into the existing United Nations educational framework.

Another major priority is *increasing public awareness*. There remains a considerable lack of awareness of the interrelatedness of all human activities and the environment, due to inaccurate or insufficient information. Developing countries in particular lack relevant technologies and expertise. Public sensitivity to environment and development problems must be increased, along with a sense of personal responsibility and greater motivation and commitment towards sustainable development.

Countries should strengthen and establish advisory bodies to act as catalysts for public environment and development information. They should promote a cooperative relationship with the media, entertainment and advertising industries and initiate discussions to mobilize their experience in shaping public behaviour and consumption patterns. In raising public awareness, modern communication technologies should be utilized to ensure that all sectors of society are being reached. Environment-related leisure and tourism activities should be supported, such as museums, zoos and national parks. Public awareness should be heightened regarding the impacts of violence in society. The educational establishment, particularly the tertiary sector, should be encouraged to contribute more to overall awareness-building. Non-governmental organizations should increase their involvement through joint awareness initiatives and improved interchange with other sectors of society. Countries should increase their interaction with indigenous people and their communities and develop support programmes for women, children and youth. The United Nations should improve its channels of outreach and interaction with Governments in the above activities.

A third priority is *promoting training* to develop human resources to facilitate the transition to a more sustainable world. This should have a job-specific focus, aimed at filling lacunae in knowledge and skills that would help individuals find employment, increase productivity and, at the same time, address environment and development needs.

Countries, with the support of the United Nations, should identify workforce and training needs and integrate environmental and development issues into current training curricula. They should encourage all sectors of society, such as industries and universities, to include an environmental management component in relevant training activities. Countries should also establish or strengthen practical training programmes for graduates from vocational schools, high schools and universities in order to enable them to meet labour market requirements and achieve sustainable livelihoods. Together with industry, trade unions and consumer groups, Governments should promote an understanding of the interrelationships between good environment and good business practices.

Sustainable development education requires the training of teachers, scientists, the business community, government officials and members of society on basic sustainable development concepts, based on up-to-date information. In building capacities and developing human resources, the identification of sector-specific training programs is important.

For all the above educational activities, additional funding is essential, although much could be done through the reallocation of existing funds, the lifting of restrictions on private schooling, better use of existing facilities, training arrangements and increasing community contributions.

7.2 STRENGTHENING THE ROLE OF MAJOR GROUPS

An essential element for the successful implementation of Agenda 21 is the active and full participation of all relevant groups, including women, youth, indigenous people and their communities, non-governmental organizations, farmers, local authorities, trade unions, business and industry and the science and technology community. The diverse backgrounds, skills and experiences these groups can offer are essential to the transition to sustainable development.

7.2.1 *Global action for women towards sustainable and equitable development*

Ensuring sustainable development requires women's empowerment and their full, equal and beneficial involvement in decision-making processes as well as their full participation as planners, managers, scientists and technical advisers in all activities related to environmental management and sustainable development.

To this end, the Rio Conference reaffirmed the Nairobi Forward Looking Strategies for the Advancement of Women, which recognized the important linkages between women's roles in development and protection of the environment and adopted measures to enhance women's participation in national ecosystem management and control of environmental degradation. Essential to women's full participation in ecosystem management and sustainable development is the elimination of all constitutional, legal, administrative, cultural, educational, social, behavioral and attitudinal obstacles. The Conference endorsed measures to ratify, implement, enforce and review the Convention on the Elimination of All Forms of Discrimination against Women to meet environment and development objectives. The effective implementation of the 1990 World Declaration on the Survival, Protection and Development of Children and its Plan of Action were also endorsed as essential for sustainable development in view of their implications for the girl child and the teenage girl.

One of the most important objectives of this programme for *global action for women towards sustainable and equitable development* is the formulation and implementation of clear governmental policies and national guidelines, strategies and plans for the achievement of equality in all aspects of society. This would include the promotion of women's literacy, education, training, nutrition and health and their participation in key decision-making positions and in management of the environment, particularly as it pertains to their access to resources by facilitating better access to all forms of credit, particularly in the informal sector, and taking measures to ensure women's access to property rights as well as agricultural inputs and implements.

A key priority activity in this programme is advancing women's role in sustainable development and environmental management by enhancing their human resource capacities through their equal education and training at all levels and in all fields in rural and urban areas, their participation and intellectual contributions to the productive spheres of society and their contribution to promoting sustainable consumption patterns and environmentally sound development. Governments are urged to take steps to increase the number of women decision makers, planners, managers and technical advisors in the fields of environment and development. They are also urged to implement legal and administrative reform measures to ensure the full and equal participation of women in sustainable development and all aspects of public life. They should also enact measures to reduce women's workloads and improve women's access to land, clean water, fuel and other resources, such as banking facilities, particularly in rural areas. International organizations should work to feature women more prominently in programmes and decision-making related to environment and development.

Programme elements also contain activities which ensure that persistent negative images, stereotypes and prejudices against women must be eliminated, as well as acts of violence against women. Steps should be taken to promote women's literacy, education, women-centred and women-managed health care and family planning facilities, day care centres and equitable employment opportunities. Programmes should also be developed to raise consumer awareness and promote the active participation of women to achieve changes in consumption and production patterns. Women's knowledge and experience of sustainable development must be researched and the results incorporated into development planning. The impact of armed hostilities, structural adjustment policies and environmental degradation on women must also be the focus of research. A multi-dimensional approach is required to promote measures to strengthen and empower women's bureaux, women's non-governmental organizations and women's groups in capacity-building.

A section entitled "Areas Requiring Urgent Action" was also adopted which called for urgent action in certain areas to avert the ongoing rapid environmental and economic degradation in developing countries that generally affect the lives of women and children in rural areas. These include drought, desertification, deforestation, armed hostilities, natural disasters, toxic waste and the aftermath of the use of unsuitable agro-chemical products.

7.2.2 *Children and youth in sustainable development*

Youth, those between 14 and 30 years of age, comprise nearly 30 per cent of the world's population. The majority of today's youth—numbering over 1.2 billion in developing countries—face a difficult future, since their very basic needs are often not adequately met when they are children, thus leaving them underequipped for adult life. For example, a mere 23 per cent of the world's youth complete secondary education, only 9 per cent of whom live in developing countries. In the industrial world, youth unemployment has jumped faster than any other sector in society, presently reaching levels well over 28 per cent in some countries.

Youth, who are destined to inherit the world, need to be accorded the right to a secure and healthy future. They have unique perspectives and an ethical and moral drive that could potentially alter many of society's inequities and environmentally degrading patterns. It is critical that youth be allowed to participate in the decision-making process. Moreover, youth must have access to education, training and subsequent employment and livelihood opportunities to enable them to lead better lives and contribute to environmental protection and sustainable economic and social development.

In *advancing the role of youth and actively involving them in the protection of the environment and the promotion of economic and social development,* Governments should set up or assist existing national mechanisms, including youth committees, task forces, youth non-governmental organizations and advisory councils to promote dialogue and enable their participation in decision-making processes at local, regional and national levels. All Member States should ensure youth participation in appropriate Government delegations. All youth must be ensured access to secondary education and vocational training that incorporates concepts of environmental awareness and sustainable development: national Governments should provide employment and remunerative earning opportunities for youth on completion of their basic education and training.

There are numerous and excellent efforts, relevant to sustainable development and environmental protection, that have been developed by the young for the young. These are underway globally and need the recognition and support of Governments and other sectors of society.

Children will inherit the responsibility for looking after the Earth. In many developing countries, children make up nearly half of the population. Children are highly vulnerable to the effects of environmental degradation and their specific interests need to be taken fully into account in implementing Agenda 21. Governments should implement programmes for *children in sustainable development,* in particular in health, nutrition, education, literacy, poverty alleviation and primary environmental care. Specifically, they should ratify the Convention on the Rights of the Child, which addresses each child's basic needs. There is a need to expand educational opportunities and establish methods that incorporate children's concerns into all levels of policy relating to environment and development. The United Nations, along with other intergovernmental and non-governmental agencies, should collaborate with the United Nations Children's Fund (UNICEF) and other relevant organizations to develop programmes for children.

7.2.3 *Recognizing and strengthening the role of indigenous people and their communities*

Indigenous people and their communities represent a significant percentage of the global population. They have a historic relationship with their lands, including the environment of the areas which they traditionally occupy, and are generally descendants of the original inhabitants of those lands. They have, over many generations, developed a holistic traditional scientific knowledge of their lands, natural resources and the environment. Their ability, however, to participate fully in sustainable development has tended to be limited as a result of economic, social and historical factors.

In view of the interrelationship between the natural environment, its sustainable development and the cultural, social, economic and physical well-being of indigenous people, national and international efforts to implement environmentally sound and sustainable development should also work at *recognizing and strengthening the role of indigenous people and their communities*.

In full partnership with indigenous people and their communities, Governments and international bodies should establish a process to empower indigenous people in order that they may both share in the benefits of and contribute their traditional knowledge and experience to sustainable development. The lands of indigenous people should be protected from activities that are either environmentally unsound or considered by the indigenous people and their communities to be socially and culturally inappropriate. Their traditional values, knowledge and environmental resource management practices, including the unique experience of indigenous women, should be recognized and promoted as valuable contributions to sustainable development. The traditional and direct dependence of indigenous people and their communities on renewable resources and ecosystems, including sustainable harvesting, should be recognized as a factor essential to their well-being. National dispute-resolution arrangements relating to settlement of land and resource-management concerns should be developed and strengthened. Capacity-building for indigenous people and their communities should be enhanced, based on the adaptation and exchange of traditional experience, knowledge and resource management practices. In addition, indigenous people and their communities should receive support for alternative environmentally sound means of production to ensure a range of choices on how to improve their quality of life. Research and education programmes should be strengthened to achieve a wider and improved understanding of indigenous people's knowledge and management experience related to the environment and its application to contemporary development challenges.

The active participation of indigenous people and their communities in the formulation of national policies, laws and programmes relating to resource management, conservation strategies and other development processes affecting them should be strengthened, including their initiation of proposals for such policies. Indigenous people should also be involved in the programmes established by international organizations and Governments to support and review sustainable development strategies.

7.2.4 *Strengthening the role of non-governmental organizations: partners for sustainable development*

Non-governmental organizations (NGOs) play a vital role in shaping and implementing participatory democracy. Independence is one of their major attributes and is the precondition of real participation. The credibility of NGOs lies in the responsible and constructive role they play in society. The NGOs, along with the non-profit organizations representing major social groups, possess well-established and diverse expertise in fields which will be of particular importance to the implementation and monitoring of environmentally sound, socially responsible and sustainable development.

Formal and informal organizations as well as grassroots movements should, therefore, be recognized as partners in the implementation of Agenda 21. The formidable global network of NGOs, operating at the international, national and local levels, should be tapped, enabled and strengthened towards this end. Governments, international bodies and society at large should develop mechanisms to allow them to play their partnership role responsibly and effectively, including in the conception, establishment and evaluation of official mechanisms designed to review the implementation of sustainable development programmes.

For its part, the United Nations system should initiate a process, in consultation with NGOs, to review formal procedures for their involvement at all levels including policy design, decision-making, implementation and evaluation of programmes. The United Nations system should also review its financial and administrative support to NGOs, as well as the extent and effectiveness of NGO involvement in implementing projects and programmes of the United Nations.

At the national and local level, Governments should establish or enhance an existing dialogue with NGOs and their self-organized networks to recognize and strengthen their respective roles in implementing sustainable development. This dialogue would serve to efficiently channel integrated NGO inputs to the governmental policy development process, and facilitate non-governmental coordination in implementing national policies at the programme level. The involvement of NGOs in national mechanisms to implement sustainable development should make the best use of their particular capacities, especially in the fields of education, public awareness, poverty alleviation and environmental protection and rehabilitation.

To ensure that the full potential contribution of NGOs as partners in sustainable development is realized, the fullest possible communication and cooperation between them, international organizations and national and local Governments is essential. This includes the need to make available to NGOs the data and information necessary for their effective contribution to research and to the design, implementation and evaluation of programmes.

NGOs should also foster cooperation and communication among themselves to reinforce their effectiveness as actors in the implementation of sustainable development.

7.2.5 *Strengthening the role of farmers*

Farming is the central activity of much of the world's population. While the past 20 years have shown impressive gains in agricultural production, this increase in some cases, especially in Africa, has not been able to keep up with population growth and increasing food demand.

Faced with limited access to technology and alternative livelihood, farmers in developing countries are often forced to overexploit their land, inevitably leading to the loss of soil fertility and lower crop yields. If agriculture is to meet future food demands in the decades ahead, farmers worldwide should be able to adopt practices that are both highly productive and sustainable.

A farmer-centred approach that emphasizes participatory methods in research, extension and development is the key to implementing sustainable agricultural and rural development. Since farmers' livelihoods are intimately tied to the land upon which they toil, ensuring a decentralized decision-making process through the creation and strengthening of local organizations in order to delegate more authority and responsibility would give them the necessary incentives to invest and utilize their land sustainably. Supporting the formation of farmers' organizations through the provision of legal frameworks is crucial to the decentralization process.

Governments should promote farming practices and technologies that would increase the productivity of land in a sustainable way. Governments should adopt legal and administrative measures to protect and formalize the right of women farmers to land, technology, inputs and training and to remove remaining sexual biases from agrarian and development policy. National, regional and international organizations involved in agricultural development and research should allow for the direct participation of farmers and their representatives in their deliberations and in developing location-specific, environment-friendly farming techniques.

Governments should also support trade policies, agricultural input price levels, fiscal incentives and other policy instruments that take into account farming's true environmental cost and encourage farmers to utilize their land, water and forest resources in both a more productive and sustainable manner. They should also strengthen farmer movements and institutions at the community level which are dealing with resource management.

Governments and farmer organizations should work to document, synthesize and disseminate development project experiences, so as to make use of the lessons of the past when formulating and implementing policies affecting farmers. They should establish networks to exchange low-cost, sustainable farming techniques, and develop pilot projects and extension services that would seek to build on the traditional knowledge of all farmers.

7.2.6 *Local authorities' initiatives in support of Agenda 21*

Local authorities construct, operate and maintain economic, social and environmental infrastructures, oversee planning processes, establish local environmental policies and regulations and assist in implementing national and sub-national environmental policies. As the level of governance closest to the people, they play a vital role in educating and mobilizing the public for sustainable development.

Each local authority should enter into a dialogue with its citizens, local organizations and private enterprises and adopt a local community Agenda 21 environmental and developmental action plan particularly suited to local problems, opportunities and values. By consulting and developing a consensus among these groups, local authorities are ideally placed to acquire relevant and timely information. This process of consultation would also increase household and individual awareness of sustainable development issues. Local authorities in each country should be encouraged to implement and monitor programmes which aim to ensure that women and youth are represented in decision-making, planning and implementation processes.

The associations of cities and other local authorities should increase their cooperation and coordination with the goal of enhancing the exchange of information and experience among local authorities. Local authority programmes, policies, laws and regulations to achieve Agenda 21 objectives should be assessed and modified, based on adopted local programmes.

In addition, funding should be mobilized for local authority programmes, particularly through existing institutions working in the field of local authority capacity-building and local environment management. Partnerships should be fostered among relevant agencies, such as the United Nations Development Programme (UNDP), the United Nations Centre for Human Settlements (UNCHS/Habitat), the United Nations Environment Programme (UNEP), the World Bank, regional banks, the International Union of Major Metropolises, the Summit of Great Cities of the World, the United Towns Organization and other relevant international partners, with a view to mobilizing increased international support for local authority programmes. An important goal should be to support, extend and improve existing institutions working in the field of local authority capacity-building and local environment management. Such a sectoral consultation would complement concurrent country-focused mobilization of international funds and assistance.

Local authorities themselves, through representatives of their associations, should be encouraged to establish processes to increase the exchange of information, experience and mutual technical assistance within and among countries.

7.2.7 Strengthening the role of workers and their trade unions

Trade unions, with their massive global membership, necessarily feature strongly in the quest for sustainable development. Given their central role in addressing industrial issues, trade unions can make an important contribution to the protection of the environment and the promotion of equitable social development. Through their collaborative networks and extensive membership, trade unions are ideally placed to channel and promote the concepts and practices of sustainable development.

In order for trade unions to play a full and informed role in support of sustainable development, Governments and employers must respect and promote the rights of individual workers to freely associate and organize, as laid down in the Conventions of the International Labour Organisation (ILO). Governments should ratify and implement these Conventions. Within this context, trade unions and employers can and should jointly establish a common framework for environmental policy, and set priorities for improving the working environment and the overall environmental-developmental performance of their enterprises.

Trade unions should continue to define, develop and promote policies on all aspects of sustainable development, both independently and in cooperation with international and regional organizations. At the workplace, they should participate in environmental audits and should be given access to adequate training to augment their environmental awareness, ensure their safety and health and improve their economic and social welfare, particularly with respect to the rights and status of women in the workplace. In their communities, trade unions should participate in local environment and development activities, including environmental impact assessments, and promote joint action on potential problems of common concern.

For their part, Governments should ensure that trade unions are able to participate actively in decisions on the design, implementation and evaluation of national and international policies and programmes on environment and development, including employment policies, industrial strategies, labour adjustments programmes and technology transfers.

The established principles of tripartism provide a basis for strengthened collaboration between workers and their representatives, and Governments and their employers, in the equitable implementation of sustainable development. With additional resources, the ILO should play an extended role in supporting these activities.

7.2.8 *Strengthening the role of business and industry*

Business and industry, including transnational corporations, play a major role in the social and economic development of a country. Business and industry is taken to mean all manufacturing, mining, utilities, services and commerce, formal and informal, private and public and operating nationally and internationally. These enterprises, producing many goods and services that improve human welfare, are also important in providing employment and livelihood opportunities. The policies and operations of business and industry, including its research and development of new and innovative processes and products, can also greatly help reduce impacts of resource use and promote environmentally sound and sustainable development.

Enterprises are starting to recognize that environmental management is a priority and are implementing policies that are environmentally and socially responsible, through increasingly voluntary initiatives. Regulatory policies and the growing consciousness of consumers have also, to a large extent, contributed in many countries to improved environmental and social responsibility in the business and industry sector.

One priority for business and industry is *promoting cleaner production* systems through technologies and processes that utilize resources more efficiently while producing less wastage. This requires mechanisms to facilitate and encourage innovation, competition and voluntary initiatives that, in turn, would promote more varied, efficient and effective options.

There is also a need to reduce or eliminate the inefficient use of resources, the wastes of which have many negative social and environmental impacts. The concept of cleaner production technologies implies striving for optimal efficiencies at all stages of a product's life cycle. The aim of such actions is to increase the efficiency of resource utilization, expand the reuse and recycling of residues and reduce the quantity of waste discharge per unit of economic output.

A second priority is *promoting responsible entrepreneurship*. Entrepreneurship is an important driving force for innovation, increasing market efficiencies and responding to challenges and opportunities. Small and medium entrepreneurs play a very important role in the social and economic development of a country. Often, they are the major means for rural development, generating off-farm employment and other remunerative activities. Responsible entrepreneurship can greatly improve the efficiency of resource use, reduce risks and hazards, minimize wastes and safeguard environmental qualities.

Governments, in partnership with business and industry, need to facilitate the establishment and operations of business and industry through measures such as efficient administration and regulation and economic incentives. Consumers, the public at large, workers, trade unions, the scientific and technological community and other major groups should also take part in the development of environmentally sound business and industry.

7.2.9 *Scientific and technological community*

The scientific and technological community, with its enormous capacity for generating possible solutions to the many problems which face us today, can greatly contribute to environmentally sound and sustainable development. Yet its potential has been far from fully realized, due in large part to insufficient communication. It is imperative that links between this valuable human resource and both decision makers and the public be expanded and strengthened.

Improving communication and cooperation among the scientific and technological community and decision makers and the public can help implement more effective strategies for environmentally sound and sustainable development, on the basis of the best available knowledge. At the same time such cooperation would assist the scientific and technological community in developing priorities for research and for proposing constructive solutions.

National scientific and technological activities should be more responsive to sustainable development needs as part of an overall effort to strengthen national research and development systems. In this respect, the membership of national scientific and technological advisory councils, organizations and committees should be strengthened and widened, with the particular aim of making them more representative of the various strands of public opinion. Mechanisms should be developed for increasing scientific input into international collaborative and negotiating processes towards international agreements. Scientific and technological advice should be heard at the highest levels of Governments and intergovernmental organizations.

Scientific and technological professionals at universities, research institutions and other centres of knowledge bear a special responsibility to disseminate their results, not only to peers in other fields but also to decision makers and the general public as well; those active in this respect should be recognized and supported. National scientific research reports that are understandable and relevant to local needs are an excellent example of how the scientific and technological community could better serve society. Links between the official scientific and technological sector and industry need to be improved. Mechanisms for disseminating information on sustainable development should also be established. Furthermore, the role of women in the scientific and technological disciplines must be promoted and strengthened.

An important need is the *promotion of codes of practice and guidelines* in order for the scientific and technological community to best advise the development process. A broader and more extensive national and international effort should develop a full range of codes of practice and guidelines regarding sustainable development, and take into account the Rio Declaration on Environment and Development. This would involve reviewing and amending relevant national and international environment and development legal instruments to ensure that this new ethos is reflected in regulatory machinery, as well as the establishment and strengthening of national advisory groups focusing on environmental and developmental ethics. Their integration into national research priorities and education and training curricula is, therefore, necessary. Fundamentally, these codes of practice and guidelines should mirror the changing global society.

IV

*Agenda 21:
The Essential Means*

AGENDA 21:
THE ESSENTIAL MEANS

THE achievement of the objectives of Agenda 21 calls for a global partnership for sustainable development where all nations will need to make political, social and economic commitments, both individually and globally, to ensure the allocation of essential means for a viable and sustainable human future. These means include making available the necessary information and data for decision-making, national capacity-building, science for sustainable development and environmentally sound technology, international legal instruments, institutional arrangements and financial resources and mechanisms.

Access to requisite information, for both decision makers and the general public, is indispensable in the efforts toward sustainable development. The integration of environment and development should be reflected in a reorientation of attitudes, in changes in decision-making and in the data and information systems for planning, implementation and monitoring.

The ability of a country to make the transition to sustainable development is dependent to a large extent on its endogenous institutional and professional capacity. Strengthen-

The essential means

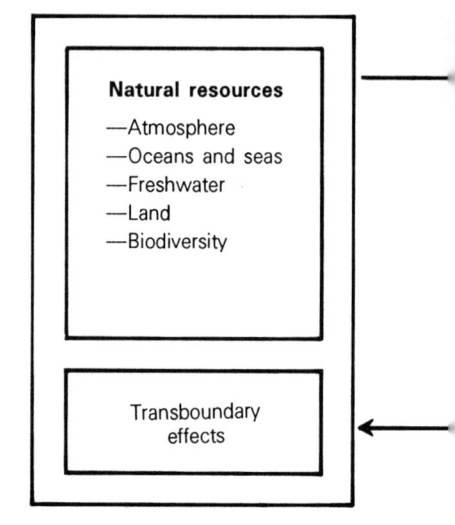

```
┌─────────────────────────────┐
│  ┌───────────────────────┐  │
│  │ **Natural resources** │  │──→
│  │ —Atmosphere           │  │
│  │ —Oceans and seas      │  │
│  │ —Freshwater           │  │
│  │ —Land                 │  │
│  │ —Biodiversity         │  │
│  │                       │  │
│  └───────────────────────┘  │
│  ┌───────────────────────┐  │
│  │     Transboundary     │  │←──
│  │        effects        │  │
│  └───────────────────────┘  │
└─────────────────────────────┘
```

Driving forces
- Value systems and lifestyles
- Population (urban and rural)
- Socio-economic system
- Knowledge

Production
- Energy
- Agriculture
- Water supply
- Industry
- Services
- Transportation
- Forestry
- Fisheries
- Mining

Consumption
- Level
- Resource intensity
- Food
- Energy
- Water
- Materials
- Other services

Environmental effects
- Depletion of natural resource stocks
- Land degradation and pollution
- Growing fragility of ecosystems
- Air, water and marine pollution
- Toxic hazardous and solid waste
- Loss of biodiversity
- Threats to life-support systems

Human welfare
- Present and future generations

Agenda 21
Essential means

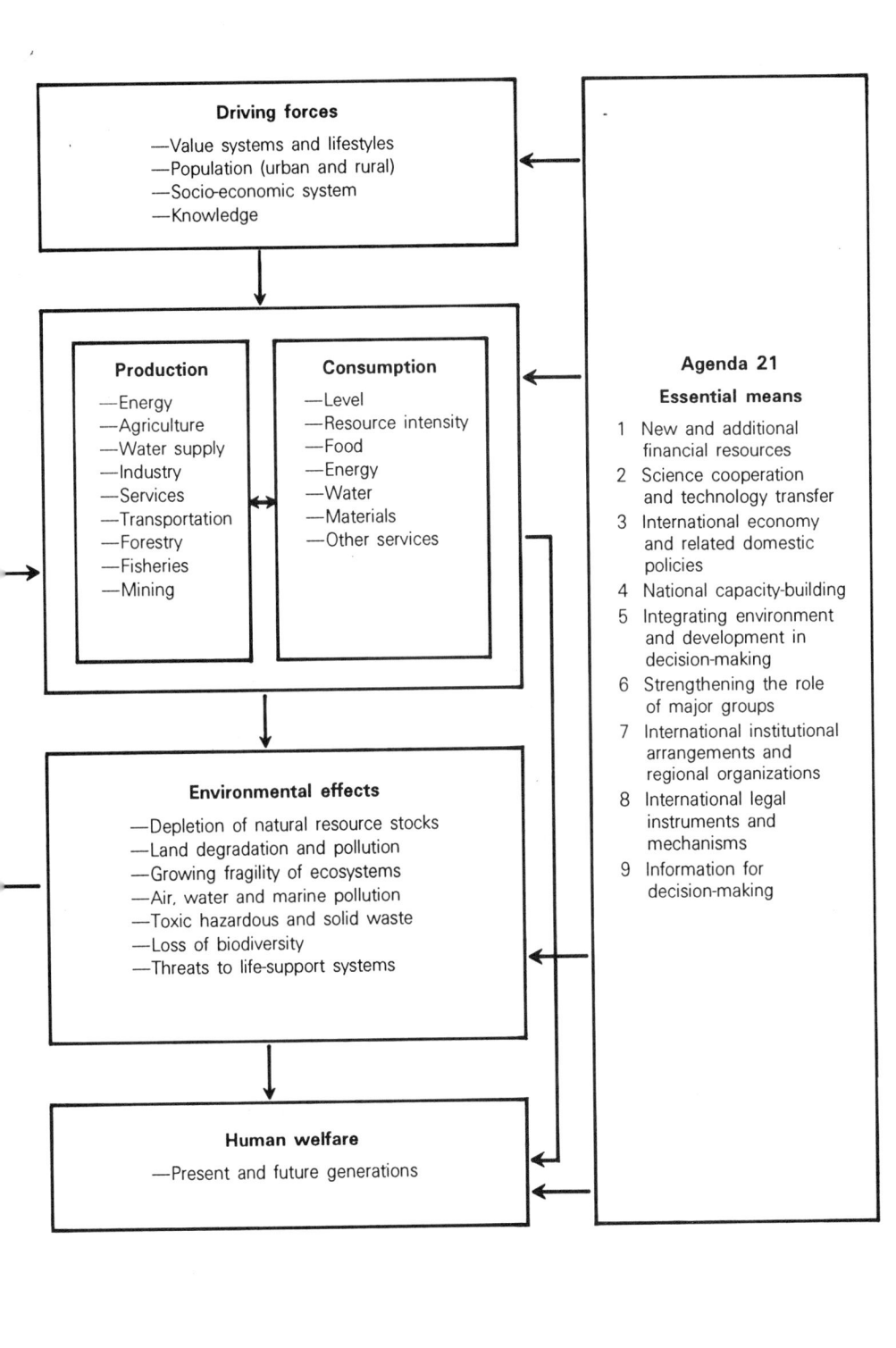

1. New and additional financial resources
2. Science cooperation and technology transfer
3. International economy and related domestic policies
4. National capacity-building
5. Integrating environment and development in decision-making
6. Strengthening the role of major groups
7. International institutional arrangements and regional organizations
8. International legal instruments and mechanisms
9. Information for decision-making

ing these national capacities is a central element of all Agenda 21 programmes. National capacity-building represents a challenge for both developing and industrialized countries alike.

The industrially advanced countries have, over time, built up a substantial base of scientific and technological knowledge that should be shared with the developing world to ensure a rapid transition to environmentally sound and sustainable development. At the same time, the indigenous knowledge and cultural heritage of developing countries must also be integrated with modern knowledge and technology.

International and legal agreements dealing with environmental matters are essential to ensure coverage, participation and compliance with regard to sustainable development and environmental security. The special needs and concerns of developing countries in this respect, often inadequately covered in the past, require priority attention.

The successful implementation of Agenda 21 necessitates modification and strengthening of the relevant institutional arrangements at national, subregional, regional and international institutional levels. This concerns both the United Nations system as well as intergovernmental and non-governmental organizations and the private sector.

The developmental and environmental objectives of Agenda 21 will require a substantial flow of new and additional financial resources to developing countries to enable them to achieve environmentally sound and sustainable development and participate fully in international environmental cooperation.

8

INFORMATION FOR DECISION-MAKING

SUSTAINABLE development requires the availability of accurate and timely information to help decision makers and the general public make sound decisions.

In sustainable development, everyone inevitably makes decisions and both uses and provides information, such as data, knowledge and experience. The need for information arises everywhere, from national and international to grassroots and individual levels. While considerable information already exists, more and different types of information need to be collected at local, regional and global scales, in order to assess the state and evolution of important ecosystem, natural resource, pollution and socio-economic variables.

The gap in the availability, quality, coherence, standardization and accessibility of data between the developed and developing world has been increasing, seriously impairing the capacities of countries to make informed decisions concerning environment and development. *Bridging the data gap* is essential to ensure that decisions are based increasingly on sound information.

Within many developing countries, and also at the international level, there is a general lack of capacity to access, collect and analyze information and disseminate relevant and timely information to users. Furthermore, there is a need for improved coordination between environmental and developmental data and information activities, especially in the context of sustainability.

Many commonly recorded indicators generally do not adequately cover the attributes of sustainability. In many instances, methods for assessing the interactions between different sectoral environmental and developmental parameters are insufficiently developed or applied. As a result, the information base often cannot adequately support decision-making towards sustainable and well-integrated environment and development systems.

Many countries are very far from being able to collect all the data required for decision-making. A number of developing countries lack the resources to undertake such programmes. At the international level, the situation is not much better, while at the regional level, even among the most economically advanced countries, much relevant information is lacking. Available data at the global level is not comprehensive.

Sustainable development indicators need to be developed to provide a solid base for decision-making at all levels, and so contribute to a self-regulatory sustainable and integrated environment and development system. These indicators should be developed through a consultative process and should capture the complex linkages between the environmental, economic and social features of natural and human systems. The existing information collection activities of Earthwatch should be strengthened, especially in the areas of urban air, freshwater and land resources, including forests, rangeland, other habitats and soil degradation, biodiversity and global atmosphere. Special attention must be paid to collecting information on population dynamics, poverty, health and vulnerable groups, such as women, youth and indigenous people and their communities, and on the relationships between these issues and the environment.

International organizations involved in the above sectoral information collection activities should strengthen and develop guidelines for coordinated, harmonized national and international data collection and assessment that make use of new data collection techniques, including data from satellite-based remote sensing, geographic information systems, systems models and a variety of other techniques. National Governments, together with international organizations, should establish mechanisms to help local communities sustainably manage their environment and resources by providing them and other resource users with the information and methodologies they need, including, where appropriate, traditional and indigenous knowledge and approaches.

Improving information availability, generated at the national, regional and international levels, involves strengthening existing national and international capacities of information processing, exchange and related technical assistance. It requires Governments, together with international organizations, to review and reform their national, regional and international information systems and services in sectors related to sustainable development, with an emphasis on transforming existing information into forms better suited for decision-making.

An important consideration for providing timely and relevant details and information on all critical aspects of sustainable development would be that it would make the process transparent and widely facilitate expert and public participation. These aspects would bring to the fore any important elements that may have been left out in the initial planning and thus improve the overall scope and successful implementation of the measures. Creative approaches must be developed to ensure that the overwhelming volume of data and information required to address the wide range of sectoral and cross-sectoral issues within sustainable development is properly documented and shared. Governments should encourage networking and coordinating mechanisms among non-governmental organizations, bilateral donors, the private sector and the public at large for sharing information on sustainable development projects.

9

NATIONAL MECHANISMS AND INTERNATIONAL COOPERATION FOR CAPACITY-BUILDING

A country's ability to follow the path to a sustainable society is determined to a large extent by its endogenous capacity to make independent and equitable decisions compatible with sustainable development regarding needs, priorities and viable strategies. This capacity encompasses the country's human, technical, organizational, institutional and resource capabilities to choose and implement actions and development options, which are determined in part by the public's perceived needs and by environmental potentials and limits. In varying degrees, all countries need to build endogenous capacities to enhance their ability to effectively respond to a wide range of development and environment issues.

Developing countries would take the lead in building their capacities to accelerate environmentally sound and sustainable development. National experts would carefully assess their country's economic capacity weaknesses. This national assessment, carried out with the active participation of relevant government departments, non-governmental organizations, academics and the public, would reflect each country's particular geographic, environmental and cultural context and the available resources for development, national aspirations and social, economic and developmental needs. It would identify requirements at national, regional and international levels. This approach would be helpful to donors, as it would allow them to develop, over time, the specific capacities and services needed to help address each country's unique sustainable development needs.

This assessment would form the basis of a national capacity-building action plan in partnership with the international donor community. External support would be sought selectively and integrated into the action plan, fitting it into in a larger, coordinated set of national measures. The international community must be willing to adopt a new integrated services approach to assistance, and move away from the diverse and fragmented help that may reflect its own views of sustainable development priorities, not the recipient's.

This integrated approach would place sustainable development on the centre stage, providing a balance to existing programmes that tend to take a country-by-country approach. To ensure coherence and consistency of action, United Nations agencies are called upon to establish joint assistance programmes with other multilateral, regional and non-governmental groups to address these linked environment and development needs. The United Nations Development Programme (UNDP), which already coordinates the country programming process of the agencies of the United Nations, would play a major role in this effort.

Strengthening endogenous capacity requires a combination of national effort and cooperative partnerships with the international community, industry and non-governmental organizations. Technical cooperation can enrich a whole range of human resources development activities by improving the skills, knowledge, technical know-how and productive attitudes needed to identify priorities, formulate strategies and policies and implement programmes for sustainable development.

Building, developing and managing national and regional capacities would feature an ongoing participatory process that works to reconcile national needs, priorities, constraints and opportunities with the programmatic proposals of Agenda 21. Reorienting the nature of developmental assistance and technical cooperation would involve the coordination of aid programmes, the participation of all interest groups and the modification and strengthening of institutional structures to deal with long-term challenges over providing short-term assistance to solve immediate problems. Priority activities will vary from country to country, as dictated by economic, cultural and other criteria. Consensus at the national level would greatly aid the formulation of strategies for implementing Agenda 21.

Governments would identify national capacity sources and present their technical cooperation needs in a framework of sector strategies. Developing country technical cooperation arrangements with international organizations and donor institutions would be on the basis of long-term capacity-building strategies that elaborate the policy changes to be implemented, budgetary issues, networking arrangements among institutions, human resource requirements, technology and equipment requirements, public and private sector needs and educational and research programmes.

Donor and recipient countries, the organizations and institutions of the United Nations system and international public and private organizations will have to review aid and technical cooperation programmes with regard to: evaluating existing capacity for environment and development project management, including technical and institutional abilities;

assessing the contribution of existing technical cooperation activities to build up long-term national capacity; adapting a participatory approach that includes municipalities, non-governmental organizations, universities, research centres and the private sector; ensuring the availability of recurrent expenditures and human resource and institutional capacities to sustain the effective use of capital investment; and improving the aid process by giving greater attention to capacity-building strategies for environment and development programmes, both in country-related coordination processes, such as consultative groups and round tables, and in sectoral coordination mechanisms.

At the regional level, existing organizations will have to consider improving regional and subregional consultative processes to facilitate the exchange of data, information and experience.

10

SCIENCE FOR SUSTAINABLE DEVELOPMENT

SCIENCE is essential for the prudent management of the Earth's environment and utilization of its resources. The global life-support system is threatened with unprecedented environmental changes which, if unchecked, could seriously impair human development. These threats require major preventive and corrective actions, drawing on interdisciplinary scientific research to improve our knowledge and understanding of land, oceans, atmosphere and their interlocking water, nutrient and biogeochemical cycles and energy flows, which all form part of the Earth's system. In the face of threats of irreversible environmental damage, lack of full scientific understanding should not be an excuse to postpone actions which are justified in their own right. The precautionary approach could provide a basis for policies relating to complex systems that are not yet fully understood and whose consequences of disturbances cannot yet be predicted.

Strengthening the scientific basis for sustainable management requires longer-term perspectives and policies and the integration of the local and regional effects of global environmental change into the development process. The elements of uncertainty and risk need to be incorporated in the design of robust policies, seeking to keep open a range of options to ensure flexible responses to fluctuating patterns of resource consumption, availability and sustainability.

The sciences are demonstrating the link between the concept of Earth as a life-support system with appropriate development strategies that build on its continued functioning. They are also playing an increasing role in improving the efficiency of renewable and non-renewable resource use. However, more extensive knowledge is required of the Earth's carrying capacity in the face of a rapidly changing global environment. Steps are, therefore, needed for *enhancing scientific understanding*, and will require development and greater application of the more effective and efficient analytical and predictive tools now available, such as remote sensing devices and computer modelling capabilities. National and international observation and collection research networks would be established to compile data and information for the predictive modelling and assessment of environmental changes. Another important dimension is that of the human causes and consequences of environmental change. A study of development paths that are more sustainable is essential.

Although many long-term environmental changes will likely affect people and the biosphere on a global scale, the effects at local and national levels will be profound. At the same time, human activities at local and regional levels have contributed to global threats, such as ozone depletion. This requires *improving long-term scientific assessments* at global, regional and local levels. Many countries and organizations have prepared reports on environment and development, which review current conditions and indicate future trends. Regional and global assessments could make full use of such reports, and could be broader in scope to include the results of detailed studies of future conditions under a wide range of assumptions about possible human responses, and using the best available models. It is vital that such assessments map out manageable development pathways within the environmental and socio-economic carrying capacities of each region. Full use will have to be made of traditional knowledge of local environments.

The increasingly important role the sciences must play to address environmental and development issues requires all countries, and in particular developing countries, to work towards *building up scientific capacity and capability*. The goal is to enable them to participate on an equal footing in the generation and application of the results of scientific research and development concerning sustainable development. Some of the more important ways for this are through education, training and the improvement of incentives and local infrastructures for scientific research and development. This capacity-building would also help improve public awareness and understanding of the sciences. If all countries are to participate on an equal footing in negotiations on global environmental and developmental issues, developing country scientists must be able to participate fully in relevant international scientific research programmes. The exodus of scientists from developing countries would be reduced and, in those countries where their numbers are insufficient, programmes would be initiated to increase the number of scientists.

Indigenous communities possess unique knowledge of their environment, including information on plants, animals, land and water resources and patterns of their use. These communities, including tribal and sometimes isolated populations, usually live in socially, ecologically and geographically marginal situations, and are often threatened by massive development projects or other incursions that tend to displace, and sometimes even destroy, their habitats. The traditional and local knowledge that these people have acquired over many generations would be recognized, recorded, analyzed and utilized. The constructive use of indigenous knowledge, both by itself and in combination with modern knowledge, could create new options for sustainable development.

11

TRANSFER OF ENVIRONMENTALLY SOUND TECHNOLOGY, COOPERATION AND CAPACITY-BUILDING

SUSTAINABLE development requires the world-wide development and dissemination of technologies that are both environmentally sound and safe to use. Their development would be achieved through a long-term partnership and cooperation, involving joint efforts by enterprises and Governments, as suppliers of technology, and its recipients. In such a partnership, attention would be given to the transfer of environmentally sound technologies from developed to developing countries as well as from developing to developed countries and among developing countries. Environmentally sound technologies would be compatible with nationally determined socio-economic, cultural and environmental priorities.

Environmentally sound technologies encompass total systems which include know-how, procedures, goods and services and equipment as well as organizational and managerial procedures. Human resource development, including gender considerations, and local capacity-building are, therefore, relevant aspects of technology choices.

Access and transfer of these technologies and the capacity to develop and manage them is of particular importance to developing countries. Support would be provided to build the technological capacity of developing countries so that they can make more rational choices of technology relevant to their development. Furthermore, their capability for technology assessment would be expanded, particularly with regard to full cost accounting, environmental risk evaluation and safeguards on technologies restricted or prohibited on environmental or health grounds in their home country. Regional and national scientific research, information dissemination and technology development programmes will have to be intensified. The aim is to improve technology currently used and/or replace it with environmentally sound technology. New and efficient technologies will be essential to sustaining the world's economy, protecting the environment and alleviating poverty and human suffering.

Sustainable development requires the availability, accessibility and transfer of technology and scientific information. The satisfaction of these requirements would enable informed choices and the strengthening of countries' own technological capabilities. Much of the useful technological knowledge lies in the public domain, to which developing countries can gain access, should they not be covered by patents.

The Rio Conference urged States to enhance the access to and transfer of patent-protected environmentally sound technologies, especially to developing countries, and to purchase patents and licences on commercial terms and transfer them to developing countries on non-commercial terms as part of development cooperation for sustainable development, taking into account the need to protect intellectual property. The Conference also proposed that Governments promote, facilitate and finance the access to and transfer of environmentally sound technologies and corresponding know-how, in particular to developing countries, on favourable terms, and taking account of the need to protect intellectual property rights as well as the special needs of developing countries for the implementation of Agenda 21.

It is agreed that a critical mass of research and development capacity is necessary for the effective dissemination and use of environmentally sound technologies and their local production. This includes more education and training for technologists specialized in environmentally sound technology and with an interdisciplinary outlook. Local and national culture will have to be taken into account in the development and transfer of technology.

12

INTERNATIONAL LEGAL INSTRUMENTS AND MECHANISMS

WITH well over 100 existing international agreements and instruments dealing with environmental matters, Governments find it increasingly difficult to keep up with the international regulatory process and to implement it nationally. At the same time, world-wide coverage, participation and compliance have become increasingly important to sustainable development and environmental security. The special needs and concerns of developing countries in this respect, often inadequately covered in the past, require priority attention.

As demands on the Earth's resources increase, often with global consequences, there is an increasing need to enhance the process of international treaty-making as it relates to environmental and development issues. International law on sustainable development needs to be further developed and codified overall, with special attention to the delicate balance between environmental and developmental concerns. The relationship between existing international legal instruments or agreements in the field of environment and relevant social and economic instruments or agreements requires clarification and strengthening. It is important that any negotiations in this regard be conducted on a universal basis, taking into account special circumstances in various regions. Future codification projects in this area would take into account the ongoing work of the International Law Commission of the United Nations.

At the global level, the participation in and contribution of all countries to treaty-making in the field of international law on sustainable development is essential. Yet many existing international legal instruments and agreements in the field of environment have been developed without the adequate participation and contribution of developing countries. This requires a review of such instruments and agreements in order to reflect the concerns and interests of developing countries and to ensure a balanced governance of such instruments and agreements. Developing countries would also be provided with technical assistance in their attempts to enhance their national legislative capabilities in the field of sustainable development.

The aim of the review and development of international law would be to evaluate and promote its efficacy, as well as to promote the integration of environmental and development policies through effective international instruments, or agreements, that take into account both universal principles and the differentiated needs and concerns of all countries. For example, obstacles preventing States from joining or implementing international agreements would be identified, and conflicts between environmental and social/economic agreements or instruments would be understood and prevented.

Four priority areas have been identified to meet this objective. One concerns the *review, assessment and fields of action in international law for sustainable development*, which would include as an option the continuation of the earlier practice by the United Nations Environment Programme (UNEP) of holding review meetings by government-designated experts. Another important priority area concerns the *implementation mechanisms*, such as developing efficient and practical reporting systems by parties to international agreements. A third priority area would be to work to ensure *effective participation in international law-making*, including a "head-start" support for developing countries to build up their expertise in international law, and to assure access to the necessary reference information and scientific/technical expertise. The last priority area pertains to *disputes in the field of sustainable development* and would include the further study and consideration of methods to broaden and make more effective the range of techniques available at present.

13

INTERNATIONAL INSTITUTIONAL ARRANGEMENTS

THE intergovernmental follow-up to the Rio Conference would be within the framework of the United Nations system with the General Assembly, as the highest level intergovernmental mechanism and the principal policy-making and appraisal forum, reviewing the progress of the implementation of Agenda 21, possibly in a special session no later than 1997. The Economic and Social Council (ECOSOC) would assist the General Assembly through overseeing the system-wide coordination and overview.

The nucleus of international cooperation and intergovernmental decision-making for the integration of environment and development issues, and the review and monitoring of Agenda 21 at the national, regional and international levels, would be a high-level Commission on Sustainable Development, set up in accordance with article 68 of the Charter of the United Nations. The Commission would consist of representatives of States elected as its members and provide for the active involvement of relevant intergovernmental organizations, both within and outside the United Nations system, as well as encourage the participation of non-governmental organizations. It would also be empowered with a broad set of functions related to virtually all aspects of the follow-up to the Conference, especially the systematic monitoring of the implementation of Agenda 21, and review of the financial resources available for its funding.

The focal point for inter-agency coordination within the United Nations system would be the Secretary-General in his capacity as head of the inter-agency Administrative Committee on Coordination (ACC). The ACC would also provide a vital link and interface between the multilateral financial institutions and other United Nations bodies at the highest administrative level.

The Secretary-General has been invited to make recommendations to the 47th session of the General Assembly in regard to the possible establishment of a high-level advisory board consisting of eminent persons knowledgeable about environment and development, appointed by the Secretary-General in their personal capacity. In addition, the Secretary-General will report to the General Assembly regarding provisions to be made for a highly qualified and competent Secretariat support structure within the United Nations Secretariat to provide support to the work of both intergovernmental and interagency coordination mechanisms.

In the follow-up to the Conference, in particular the implementation of Agenda 21, the role of the United Nations Environmental Programme (UNEP) and its Governing Council would need to be enhanced and strengthened. UNEP would support Governments, development agencies and other organizations in the integration of environmental aspects into their individual development policies and programmes, and promote relevant scientific research, environmental impact assessments, and techniques such as natural resource accounting and environmental economics. In addition, it would promote the development of international environmental law and provide relevant legal and institutional advice to Governments. In order for UNEP to perform these functions, it would require access to greater expertise and financial resources, as well as greater cooperation and collaboration with developmental and other relevant organs of the United Nations system.

The role of the United Nations Development Programme (UNDP) would also be crucial in the follow-up to the United Nations Conference on Environment and Development (UNCED). Through its network of field offices, it would foster the United Nations system's collective thrust in support of the implementation of Agenda 21 at the national, regional, interregional and global levels. Acting as the lead agency in organizing United Nations system efforts towards capacity-building at local, national and regional levels, it would mobilize donor resources on behalf of Governments for capacity-building in recipient countries and assist these receiving countries in establishing and strengthening their national coordination mechanisms and activities for the follow-up of UNCED.

Other United Nations bodies, such as the United Nations Conference on Trade and Development (UNCTAD), the United Nations Sudano-Sahelian Office and other specialized agencies, related organizations and relevant intergovernmental bodies, within their respective fields of competence, would play important roles in the implementation of relevant parts of Agenda 21. Also important to the successful implementation of the Agenda 21 would be the regional and subregional programmes within the United Nations system, as well as other programmes and institutions at the regional level, such as regional development banks. These programmes can work at their levels to promote capacity-building, the integration of environmental concerns in development policies and appropriate cooperation regarding transboundary issues related to sustainable development.

States have an important role to play in the follow-up to UNCED and the implementation of Agenda 21. National-level efforts need to be undertaken by all countries in an integrated manner, and policy decisions and activities at the national level—tailored to support and implement Agenda 21—need to be supported by the United Nations system upon request.

The success of the follow-up to the Rio Conference depends upon an effective link between substantive action and financial support, and this requires close cooperation and information exchange between the United Nations system and the multilateral financial organizations. Representatives of multilateral financial institutions and mechanisms, as well as the International Fund for Agricultural Development, have to be actively associated with deliberations regarding the intergovernmental structure responsible for the follow-up to Agenda 21.

The General Assembly has been invited to examine and design ways of enhancing the participation and involvement of non-governmental organizations in relation to the follow-up process to the Earth Summit. The United Nations system has been asked, in particular, to take into account the findings of non-governmental organizations' review and evaluation systems in the formulation of relevant reports of the Secretary-General concerning the implementation of Agenda 21.

14

FINANCIAL RESOURCES AND MECHANISMS

ECONOMIC growth, social development and poverty eradication are a priority in developing countries, and are essential to meet the objectives of national and global sustainability. Without the provision of financial resources and technology, developing countries would be unable to meet these goals, as embodied in Agenda 21.

It is important to note here that the non-availability of financial resources would make it impossible to implement the programmes in Agenda 21, and would void them of any significance. Also, the cost of inaction would far outweigh the total financial costs of implementing Agenda 21, and narrow the choices of future generations as well.

The secretariat of the United Nations Conference on Environment and Development has estimated that the average annual costs (1993-2000) of implementing Agenda 21 in the developing countries would be over $600 billion, including about $125 billion on grant or concessional terms from the international community. These are indicative and order of magnitude estimates only. Actual costs will depend upon the specific strategies and programmes Governments decide upon for implementation.

Agenda 21 has proposed to establish measures concerning financial resources and mechanisms, provide new and additional resources, both adequate and predictable, that permit developing countries to plan over the long term and use funding mehanisms to the full.

Official Development Assistance (ODA) would be the main source of external funding. Developed countries at the Rio Conference reaffirmed their commitments to reach the accepted United Nations target of 0.7 per cent of gross national product for ODA, and agreed to augment their aid programmes to reach that target as soon as possible and ensure the prompt implementation of Agenda 21. Some countries have agreed to reach the target by the year 2000.

The new Commission on Sustainable Development will monitor progress towards this target, and systematically review both the implementation of Agenda 21 and the availability of financial resources.

New and additional funding for sustainable development would tap all available funding sources and mechanisms. The International Development Association (IDA) could help the poorest countries meet their sustainable development objectives, as contained in Agenda 21, after examining options for funding in its 10th Replenishment. A further source of funding will be the Global Environment Facility. It would be restructured to flexibly expand its scope and coverage to the relevant programmes of Agenda 21 and ensure universal participation, transparency in governance, predictability in the flow of funds and access to these funds without introducing new forms of conditionality. Other sources of funding—on concessional or other favourable terms—to implement Agenda 21 would include regional and subregional development banks, United Nations bodies and other international organizations and specialized agencies, multilateral institutions for capacity-building and technical cooperation, bilateral assistance programmes, private funding, investment and innovative financing, drawing on debt relief, the use of economic and fiscal incentives, tradeable permits, the involvement of non-governmental organizations and the reallocation of resources committed to military purposes. Measures to address the continuing debt problems of low- and middle-income countries would be kept under review.

Developed countries have been asked to make initial financial commitments and report on such plans and commitments to the United Nations General Assembly at its forty-seventh session.

V

*Non-Legally Binding
Authoritative Statement of
Principles for a Global Consensus
on the Management,
Conservation and Sustainable
Development of All Types
of Forests*

NON-LEGALLY BINDING AUTHORITATIVE STATEMENT OF PRINCIPLES FOR A GLOBAL CONSENSUS ON THE MANAGEMENT, CONSERVATION AND SUSTAINABLE DEVELOPMENT OF ALL TYPES OF FORESTS

PREAMBLE

(*a*) The subject of forests is related to the entire range of environmental and development issues and opportunities, including the right to socio-economic development on a sustainable basis.

(*b*) The guiding objective of these principles is to contribute to the management, conservation and sustainable development of forests and to provide for their multiple and complementary functions and uses.

(*c*) Forestry issues and opportunities should be examined in a holistic and balanced manner within the overall context of environment and development, taking into consideration the multiple functions and uses of forests, including traditional uses, and the likely economic and social stress when these uses are constrained or restricted, as well as the potential for development that sustainable forest management can offer.

(*d*) These principles reflect a first global consensus on forests. In committing themselves to the prompt implementation of these principles, countries also decide to keep them under assessment for their adequacy with regard to further international cooperation on forest issues.

(e) These principles should apply to all types of forests, both natural and planted, in all geographic regions and climatic zones, including austral, boreal, subtemperate, temperate, subtropical and tropical.

(f) All types of forests embody complex and unique ecological processes which are the basis for their present and potential capacity to provide resources to satisfy human needs as well as environmental values, and as such their sound management and conservation is of concern to the Governments of the countries to which they belong and are of value to local communities and to the environment as a whole.

(g) Forests are essential to economic development and the maintenance of all forms of life.

(h) Recognizing that the responsibility for forest management, conservation and sustainable development is in many States allocated among federal/national, state/ provincial and local levels of government, each State, in accordance with its constitution and/or national legislation, should pursue these principles at the appropriate level of government.

PRINCIPLES / ELEMENTS

1

(a) "States have, in accordance with the Charter of the United Nations and the principles of international law, the sovereign right to exploit their own resources pursuant to their own environmental policies and have the responsibility to ensure that activities within their jurisdiction or control do not cause damage to the environment of other States or of areas beyond the limits of national jurisdiction".

(b) The agreed full incremental cost of achieving benefits associated with forest conservation and sustainable development requires increased international cooperation and should be equitably shared by the international community.

2

(a) States have the sovereign and inalienable right to utilize, manage and develop their forests in accordance with their development needs and level of socio-economic development and on the basis of national policies consistent with sustainable development and legislation, including the conversion of such areas for other uses within the overall socio-economic development plan and based on rational land-use policies.

(b) Forest resources and forest lands should be sustainably managed to meet the social, economic, ecological, cultural and spiritual human needs of present and future generations. These needs are for forest products and services, such as wood and wood products, water, food, fodder, medicine, fuel, shelter, employment, recreation, habitats for wildlife, landscape diversity, carbon sinks and reservoirs, and for other forest products. Appropriate measures should be taken to protect forests against harmful effects of pollution, including air-borne pollution, fires, pests and diseases, in order to maintain their full multiple value.

(c) The provision of timely, reliable and accurate information on forests and forest ecosystems is essential for public understanding and informed decision-making and should be ensured.

(d) Governments should promote and provide opportunities for the participation of interested parties, including local communities and indigenous people, industries, labour, non-governmental organizations and individuals, forest dwellers and women, in the development, implementation and planning of national forest policies.

3

(a) National policies and strategies should provide a framework for increased efforts, including the development and strengthening of institutions and programmes for the management, conservation and sustainable development of forests and forest lands.

(b) International institutional arrangements, building on those organizations and mechanisms already in existence, as appropriate, should facilitate international cooperation in the field of forests.

(c) All aspects of environmental protection and social and economic development as they relate to forests and forest lands should be integrated and comprehensive.

4

The vital role of all types of forests in maintaining the ecological processes and balance at the local, national, regional and global levels through, *inter alia*, their role in protecting fragile ecosystems, watersheds and freshwater resources and as rich storehouses of biodiversity and biological resources and sources of genetic material for biotechnology products, as well as photosynthesis, should be recognized.

5

(a) National forest policies should recognize and duly support the identity, culture and the rights of indigenous people, their communities and other communities and forest dwellers. Appropriate conditions should be promoted for these groups to enable them to have an economic stake in forest use, perform economic activities, and achieve and maintain cultural identity and social organization, as well as adequate levels of livelihood and well-being, through, *inter alia*, those land tenure arrangements which serve as incentives for the sustainable management of forests.

(b) The full participation of women in all aspects of the management, conservation and sustainable development of forests should be actively promoted.

6

(a) All types of forests play an important role in meeting energy requirements through the provision of a renewable source of bio-energy, particularly in developing countries, and the demands for fuelwood for household and industrial needs should be met through sustainable forest management, afforestation and reforestation. To this end, the potential contribution of plantations of both indigenous and introduced species for the provision of both fuel and industrial wood should be recognized.

(b) National policies and programmes should take into account the relationship, where it exists, between the conservation, management and sustainable development of forests and all aspects related to the production, consumption, recycling and/or final disposal of forest products.

(c) Decisions taken on the management, conservation and sustainable development of forest resources should benefit, to the extent practicable, from a comprehensive assessment of economic and non-economic values of forest goods and services and of the environmental costs and benefits. The development and improvement of methodologies for such evaluations should be promoted.

(d) The role of planted forests and permanent agricultural crops as sustainable and environmentally sound sources of renewable energy and industrial raw material should be recognized, enhanced and promoted. Their contribution to the maintenance of ecological processes, to offsetting pressure on primary/old-growth forest and to providing regional employment and development with the adequate involvement of local inhabitants should be recognized and enhanced.

(e) Natural forests also constitute a source of goods and services, and their conservation, sustainable management and use should be promoted.

7

(a) Efforts should be made to promote a supportive international economic climate conducive to sustained and environmentally sound development of forests in all countries, which include, *inter alia*, the promotion of sustainable patterns of production and consumption, the eradication of poverty and the promotion of food security.

(b) Specific financial resources should be provided to developing countries with significant forest areas which establish programmes for the conservation of forests including protected natural forest areas. These resources should be directed notably to economic sectors which would stimulate economic and social substitution activities.

8

(a) Efforts should be undertaken towards the greening of the world. All countries, notably developed countries, should take positive and transparent action towards reforestation, afforestation and forest conservation, as appropriate.

(b) Efforts to maintain and increase forest cover and forest productivity should be undertaken in ecologically, economically and socially sound ways through the rehabilitation, reforestation and re-establishment of trees and forests on unproductive, degraded and deforested lands, as well as through the management of existing forest resources.

(c) The implementation of national policies and programmes aimed at forest management, conservation and sustainable development, particularly in developing countries, should be supported by international financial and technical cooperation, including through the private sector, where appropriate.

(d) Sustainable forest management and use should be carried out in accordance with national development policies and priorities and on the basis of environmentally sound national guidelines. In the formulation of such guidelines, account should be taken, as appropriate and if applicable, of relevant internationally agreed methodologies and criteria.

(e) Forest management should be integrated with management of adjacent areas so as to maintain ecological balance and sustainable productivity.

(f) National policies and/or legislation aimed at management, conservation and sustainable development of forests should include the protection of ecologically viable representative or unique examples of forests, including primary/old-growth forests, cultural, spiritual, historical, religious and other unique and valued forests of national importance.

(g) Access to biological resources, including genetic material, shall be with due regard to the sovereign rights of the countries where the forests are located and to the sharing on mutually agreed terms of technology and profits from biotechnology products that are derived from these resources.

(h) National policies should ensure that environmental impact assessments should be carried out where actions are likely to have significant adverse impacts on important forest resources, and where such actions are subject to a decision of a competent national authority.

9

(a) The efforts of developing countries to strengthen the management, conservation and sustainable development of their forest resources should be supported by the international community, taking into account the importance of redressing external indebtedness, particularly where aggravated by the net transfer of resources to developed countries, as well as the problem of achieving at least the replacement value of forests through improved market access for forest products, especially processed products. In this respect, special attention should also be given to the countries undergoing the process of transition to market economies.

(b) The problems that hinder efforts to attain the conservation and sustainable use of forest resources and that stem from the lack of alternative options available to local communities, in particular the urban poor and poor rural populations who are economically and socially dependent on forests and forest resources, should be addressed by Governments and the international community.

(c) National policy formulation with respect to all types of forests should take account of the pressures and demands imposed on forest ecosystems and resources from influencing factors outside the forest sector, and intersectoral means of dealing with these pressures and demands should be sought.

10

New and additional financial resources should be provided to developing countries to enable them to sustainably manage, conserve and develop their forest resources, including through afforestation, reforestation and combating deforestation and forest and land degradation.

11

In order to enable, in particular, developing countries to enhance their endogenous capacity and to better manage, conserve and develop their forest resources, the access to and transfer of environmentally sound technologies and corresponding know-how on favourable terms, including on concessional and preferential terms, as mutually agreed, in accordance with the relevant provisions of Agenda 21, should be promoted, facilitated and financed, as appropriate.

12

(a) Scientific research, forest inventories and assessments carried out by national institutions which take into account, where relevant, biological, physical, social and economic variables, as well as technological development and its application in the field of sustainable forest management, conservation and development, should be strengthened through effective modalities, including international cooperation. In this context, attention should also be given to research and development of sustainably harvested non-wood products.

(b) National and, where appropriate, regional and international institutional capabilities in education, training, science, technology, economics, anthropology and social aspects of forests and forest management are essential to the conservation and sustainable development of forests and should be strengthened.

(c) International exchange of information on the results of forest and forest management research and development should be enhanced and broadened, as appropriate, making full use of education and training institutions, including those in the private sector.

(d) Appropriate indigenous capacity and local knowledge regarding the conservation and sustainable development of forests should, through institutional and financial support, and in collaboration with the people in local communities concerned, be recognized, respected, recorded, developed and, as appropriate, introduced in the implementation of programmes. Benefits arising from the utilization of indigenous knowledge should therefore be equitably shared with such people.

13

(a) Trade in forest products should be based on non-discriminatory and multilaterally agreed rules and procedures consistent with international trade law and practices. In this context, open and free international trade in forest products should be facilitated.

(b) Reduction or removal of tariff barriers and impediments to the provision of better market access and better prices for higher value-added forest products and their local processing should be encouraged to enable producer countries to better conserve and manage their renewable forest resources.

(c) Incorporation of environmental costs and benefits into market forces and mechanisms, in order to achieve forest conservation and sustainable development, should be encouraged both domestically and internationally.

(d) Forest conservation and sustainable development policies should be integrated with economic, trade and other relevant policies.

(e) Fiscal, trade, industrial, transportation and other policies and practices that may lead to forest degradation should be avoided. Adequate policies, aimed at management, conservation and sustainable development of forests, including, where appropriate, incentives, should be encouraged.

14

Unilateral measures, incompatible with international obligations or agreements, to restrict and/or ban international trade in timber or other forest products should be removed or avoided, in order to attain long-term sustainable forest management.

15

Pollutants, particularly air-borne pollutants, including those responsible for acidic deposition, that are harmful to the health of forest ecosystems at the local, national, regional and global levels should be controlled.

92-93210-1500
Printed in USA
Reprinted in USA
94-93047-1200